Hospitality Forever

A Sustainability Handbook
for the
Lodging Industry

Leslie E. Wildesen, Ph.D.

2010

i

Order this book online at www.trafford.com
or email orders@trafford.com

Most Trafford titles are also available at major online book retailers.

Printed in Victoria, BC, Canada.

ISBN: 978-1-4251-8596-1 (sc)

*Our mission is to efficiently provide the world's finest, most comprehensive book publishing
service, enabling every author to experience success. To find out how to publish your book, your
way, and have it available worldwide, visit us online at www.trafford.com*

Trafford rev. 5/10/2010

 www.trafford.com

North America & international
toll-free: 1 888 232 4444 (USA & Canada)
phone: 250 383 6864 ♦ fax: 812 355 4082

This book is dedicated to Chandra de Silva.

Ayubovan!

Table of Contents

Preface

I am a frequent traveler, both for work and for pleasure. I have never met a plane ticket, boat tour, elephant ride, or excursion train I didn't like. I have had the opportunity to think long and hard about the failure of the hospitality industry to understand its role in ensuring sustainable environments (and businesses) for the foreseeable future. I have seen cruise ships that were larger than the islands at which they dock; hotels that define "luxury" as the profligate waste of energy and water; tour operators who exploit the locals as workers, their villages as "attractions," and their soil and water as dumping grounds for waste.

For shame! My dictionary defines "hospitality" as "a friendly welcome and kind or generous treatment offered to guests or strangers." What are we offering to our planet and its people? Some members of the hospitality industry have begun to seek answers to this question.

Two of the first hotels in the developing world to adopt comprehensive environmental management systems that meet the international ISO 14001 standard are in Sri Lanka, a high-visibility tourist destination for Europeans and southeast Asians. Due in large part to the efforts of the Sri Lankan ISO 14001 EMS Users Association, of which Mr. Chandra de Silva was President, these two facilities volunteered to be part of a pilot project to demonstrate the efficacy of ISO 14001 to the worldwide hospitality industry, while taking the lead in creating environmentally sustainable tourism in their own country. I served as one of their consultants, with the invaluable assistance of Mr. de Silva, who owned one of the hotels in the pilot project.

This book has its origin in that experience. We all learned important lessons for the global hospitality industry, in both the developed and the developing world. Chandra and I had long discussed writing up this material together; his untimely death in June, 2008 has prevented that from happening as we had planned. But this book is a step on the path we began traveling together nearly ten years ago now, and I hope it encourages and inspires you to follow in our footsteps.

I also have had the pleasure of working with several ski areas in North America both on environmental impact assessment associated with master planning and on developing sustainability programs in line with the Sustainable Slopes charter of the National Ski Areas Association.

Whether in the tropics or the tundra, sustainability programs in the hospitality industry have certain commonalities: they are poorly understood by many hospitality managers; they can be – although they need not be – complex to launch and continue; they are usually very visible to customers, so there is a lot of pressure to succeed quickly; *and* they can pay off in immediate savings and increased customer loyalty.

Through this book I hope to help you, the hospitality business owner, manager or employee, understand sustainability programs better, begin and complete your own sustainability program, succeed under pressure, and reap the benefits of stepping onto this important pathway to sustainability.

Acknowledgements

I would especially like to thank Ray and Nansie Jubitz, formerly of the International Executive Service Corps. It was Ray's idea to launch the hotel project with Mr. de Silva under the auspices of the Technology Initiative for the Private Sector, a special IESC program in Sri Lanka. Ray, as IESC Country Director for Sri Lanka from 1999-2000, and Nansie, as Manager of Project Operations, kept the project going and made sure all necessary arrangements got made. I could not have done any of this without them, and I thank them for their support, encouragement, and friendship before, throughout, and after the project.

And of course, I want to acknowledge the support and hard work of the staff of the two pilot project hotels, without whose efforts none of this would have happened.

At Ranweli Holiday Village:
* Mr. Wimal Dassanayake, Manager
* Ms. Vivette Cooray, Manager's Secretary
* Mr. Pranith Meegama, Engineer
* Mr. Devapriya Vithanage, Accountant, and his assistant Mr. Ranjan Colombage
* Mr. Mahinda Ekanayake, Manager of the Eco-Product Department, and his able assistants Mr. Nimal Monnakulame and Mr. Samitha Harischandra
* Mr. Maxwel Buyers, Executive Chef (whose cooking demonstrations inspired us all)
* Mr. Gamini Abeysinghe, Assitant Restaurant and Bar Manager
* Mr. Harsha Jayasinghe, Front Officer Manager
* Mr. G. Abeyasinghe and Mr. Selvaraj, Housekeeping
* Mr. Washinton Fernando, Purchasing Manager
* Mr. Jayatissa Silva, Chief Supervisor

At The Lodge at Habarana:
* Mr. Sujeeva Cooray, Director and General manager, Keells Hotel Managemet Services, Ltd.
* Mr. Suraj Perera, Manager, The Lodge at Habarana
* Ms. Deepthi Amarasinghe, Coordinating Secretary and ISO 14001 project manager
* Mr. H.S. "Foni" Fonseka, Maintenance Engineer at the beginning of the project, and Mr. Nimal S. Bandara, his able replacement part way through
* Mr. Arosha Panawala, Front Office Manager and his assistant, Mr. N.V. Gamage
* Mr. Conrad de la Motte, Executive Chef, and Mr. Prasad Benittee, Executive Pastry Chef, for keeping me in garlic and onion curry and wonderful chocolate cakes!
* Mr. W. Akram, Housekeeping
* Ms. Sherine Perera, Tour Intern, for giving me a glimpse of the wonderful ancient city of Anaradhapura and the former royal capital at Kandy, and for introducing me to some of the local food delicacies at villages along the way

In the US, Grand Targhee Ski and Summer Resort, Alta, Wyoming, served as the pilot project. Not only is it vastly different in size, nature, and location from the two Sri Lankan hotels, it exists in a highly regulated atmosphere and must coordinate almost daily with federal, state and local environmental and business regulators. Special thanks go to:

* Mr. Larry Williamson, General Manager
* Ms. Sauny Sewell, Resort Naturalist

And I have to thank Mr. Kenny Abrahamson, General Manager of Loveland Ski Areas, Colorado.

I led the team that conducted the environmental impact assessment and prepared the Environmental Impact Statement for the revision of their Master Development Plan in 1994. Thanks for your hard work, Kenny. Someday I'll tell you in person that to this day I don't downhill ski, but you taught me a lot about the operational needs of a ski area, and I hope I have learned at least that much well.

Anton Camarota, my colleague and friend, is a deep thinker on sustainability and environmental management systems. He originally developed the "Five Big Questions" format for our environmental management system work with the US Environmental Protection Agency in the 1990s, which I have freely adapted to both environmental impact assessment and The Natural Step frameworks.

Lastly, thanks to Becky Goehring and Suzanne Greene, whose little red vacation cottage in Gold Beach, Oregon, served as my retreat for actually completing this manuscript. There's a cold beer in the fridge, just for you!

Leslie E. Wildesen, Ph.D.
Portland, Oregon
May 2010

Chapter 1 - Why You Need This Book

When I told a friend over dinner recently that I was working on a book about the hospitality industry, she put down her fork, leaned over the table, and said, "Do you know what I just *hate*? It's those hotels with the little laundry hang tags, telling me that if I do such-and-such they won't wash my linens. They lie! I do exactly what they tell me to, and they wash my linens anyway! What a waste of effort!"

I couldn't agree more. It *is* a waste of effort, and of time, of money, of water and energy and labor resources, of good will, of opportunity. And notice: she doesn't hate the *tags*, she hates the *hotel*, because its management enlisted her help under false pretenses. Here she was, a happy customer, willing and able to help the hotel work toward a worthwhile goal which she shares and is emotionally committed to – saving the environment – and they failed to keep their side of the agreement.

Here's another variant on the hang tag story: At a presentation I was giving on sustainability, a representative of a major North American resort told me they had stopped using hang tags because "only about 5% of their guests ever bothered to follow the instructions." When I picked my jaw up off the floor, I asked how it was they thought they could afford *not* to save 5% of their energy, water, labor and time costs? I, too, run a business, and I know that every 5% I don't have to spend drops directly to my financial bottom line, where it sits quite happily in my company's bank account.

Furthermore, when you consider that Apple has had "only" 5% of the market for personal computers for decades, which translates into millions of satisfied – no, make that enthusiastic, fanatical, evangelical – customers, how can you afford to overlook that kind of market share? This particular resort attracts thousands of international visitors every season, many of whom come from countries where such water and energy conservation practices are routine. Surely those customers must have wondered why this very well known resort seemed so backward....

Here's what this one small "hang tag" problem costs you, the hotel operator, tour director, or cruise boat captain, every day:

- ❏ By not following through on your promises, you are wasting all the money you spent on hang tags.
- ❏ By continuing to wash linens in spite of what your guests tell you they want, you are failing to earn any savings on energy, water, detergent, labor or linen replacement costs that washing fewer linens daily can provide.
- ❏ By violating the trust of your best customers, the ones who are willing to do something extra to help you succeed, you are squandering their good will, perhaps forever.
- ❏ And if you don't use hang tags at all, you are missing out on all their benefits.

And here are the longer-term implications of this one little situation for your enterprise:

- ❑ You apparently didn't learn from these failures, or even notice they were occurring, so did not take any corrective action to improve your behavior over time.
- ❑ You apparently did not take the trouble to train (or retrain) your staff, or develop a procedure that was easy for them to follow, or create incentives for following it.
- ❑ You apparently have no way to set or measure costs, earnings, return on investment, management objectives and targets, effectiveness of staff training, overall performance, quality of service, regulatory compliance, adaptability of procedures, impacts to the environment, staff efficiency and teamwork, how well you keep your promises, contribution to the community, progress toward sustainability....

One could come to believe you simply don't care about your customers, your environment, your employees, your business, your community, or your planet, because it seems you have made no systematic and sustained effort to protect, enhance, or care for any of them.

It's a wonder you are still in business!

In fact, in the context of business and environmental sustainability, this simple and all-too-common situation with hang tags is a symptom of a *major operational failure* at the practice, process, and principle levels:

- ❑ **Practice level**: The hang tag practice failed and was not either revamped or replaced with something more effective.

- ❑ **Process level**: You failed to set objectives, develop a procedure to meet them, train the staff, identify the problem when it arose, fix the problem when it was identified, learn from your mistakes, revise your objectives and retrain the staff, or monitor the system that is supposed to carry out your environmental policies. (Maybe you don't even have an environmental policy except "to comply"?)

- ❑ **Principle level**: You failed to develop or apply high-level principles to running your enterprise: How do you know you've made a good decision? How do you choose which to implement first, among competing "best practices"? Who are you, as a business? How do you operate in your community? Is it OK with you to break promises to your best customers? Do you want to have a company that can fail in this way, or do you want a self-correcting learning organization based on shared fundamental principles? What would sustainability look like, if you were to decide to go there?

All of this, of course, is the subject of this book. By the end you will have a good idea of why sustainability matters and why you should care. I will review some major hospitality industry "Best Practices" of today (we'll get to invent tomorrow's together), and give you some checklists and protocols for determining which ones you want to apply to your operations. You'll also get a set of step-by-step tools for developing an environmental management system that will keep your processes robust and effective. And you'll learn a set of science-based guiding principles to use as a compass along your pathway to business and environmental sustainability, and how to apply them to building the kind of business that will endure in the 21st century.

This is not another book that argues the merits of various definitions of sustainability, or debates how green is green, or explores the differences between ecotourism, green tourism, nature tourism, adventure tourism and mass tourism. It does not cite statistics on numbers of travelers and tourists, or amounts of money spent per person before, during, and after the trip. It does not do this because, first, any definitions or statistics are obsolete the minute they are published, and second, you already know these data by heart.

This is a book for the person in the hospitality industry who wants to make money, save money, and do the right thing: in other words, the person who wants to run a sustainable business in an environmentally sustainable way. It is for the resort operator, facility manager, or tour director who needs some solid tools for enhancing the environmental effects of his or her resort, facility, or tour. Based on real-world examples in both the developing and developed world, this book contains practical discussions, case studies, templates, checklists and protocols, resource lists, implementation tips, specific examples, diagrams and flow charts to help implement a comprehensive *system* of principles, processes, and practices to help you achieve environmental sustainability.

I believe in several basic principles, which I have tried to apply to this book:

    1.   Keep it sweet and simple.
    2.   If it ain't broke, don't fix it.
    3.   Your people are your most valuable resource.

Principle #1 is why you won't find any elaborate software programs touted here, or indeed any tools that can't be done with a simple pencil and paper and a little thought or discussion. I personally have seen organizations like yours succeed in developing sustainability programs in situations where many of the staff were illiterate; where staff members spoke 3 or more mutually unintelligible languages; where no recycling facility existed in the whole country; where the entire national power grid was shut down every afternoon so each facility had to fire up its backup generating capacity or go dark; where major roads were unpaved or so choked with traffic it took 4 hours to go less than 100 kilometers; where no tradition of collaborative management existed; where no water quality standards or testing laboratories were available; and where foreign "green" equipment, though of outstanding quality and engineering design, was prohibitively expensive.

If they can do it, you can do it.

Principle #2 means it is not necessary to dismantle programs that are already working and replace them with new, untried ones. Sustainability is an incremental thing, always adapting to the current situation, always seeking ways to enhance what is already happening. So begin where you are, add and change and shift resources as needed, measure your progress, and change course only when it will be beneficial: when it will help you reach your objectives even more easily or faster or with less cost or effort, and will benefit the planet, the people, and your bottom line.

And finally, Principle #3 leads me to ask what I think of as a very basic question: who knows more about the actual operations of your facility's kitchen, or its laundry, or its grounds keeping? the kitchen steward, launderer or groundskeeper? or the environmental manager? Think about it. Get your people involved, literally from the ground up: ask them questions, give them pencils and paper, get them into focus groups or "Green Teams" or even have the entire staff do a "dumpster dive" together (yes, even the suits) – however you can, just do it! They are the ones with the knowledge, the ideas, the energy, the motivation, and the skills to develop and then actually accomplish your sustainability program. You need their engagement and commitment: without them, you simply don't *have* a sustainability program.

This book will show you what the parts of a sustainability program look like, and how to get (or keep) going on the path. Whether you run a hotel, retirement community, cruise ship, coffee shop, tour operation, restaurant, convention center, bar, bistro, bed-and-breakfast inn, youth hostel, or dive shop, you will find something in this book you can use.

Let's begin.

Chapter 2 - What is Sustainability and Why Should You Care?

What is Sustainability?

"The golden rule for the restorative economy."

The United Nations World Commission on Environment and Development (the Brundtland Commission) in 1987 defined "sustainable development" as that which "meets the needs of the present without compromising the ability of future generations to meet their own needs."

Sustainability is forward-looking, in that it considers today's actions in light of their future effects. This is, of course, what business owners do all the time: what investments do I need to make now in order to have the business I want in 5 years? How do I need to serve my customers today in order to keep them coming back later? Which ideas, tools and strategies will best help me adapt to the changing world so I can maintain my successful enterprise?

The question changes only a bit when we add the sustainability component: What do I need to do as owner/manager/employee to ensure that the beach / forest / ski slope / reef / river / fishery our customers come to enjoy is still thriving when they visit? Put another way, how can I manage my enterprise to ensure that we are not destroying the very thing our customers come to exerience?

Paul Hawken in *The Ecology of Commerce* defines sustainability as "the golden rule for the restorative economy." Enterprises that wish to function in this new kind of economy must deliver their product or service "so it reduces consumption, energy use, distribution costs, economic concentration, soil erosion, atmospheric pollution, and other forms of environmental damage." He describes this "golden rule" as having four tasks:

> • Leave the world better than you found it
>
> • Take no more than you need
>
> • Try not to harm the environment
>
> • Make amends if you do

How did we get to these concepts, and why should you care?

The Path to Sustainability

Many kinds of organizations are learning about becoming sustainable and participating in the restorative economy. Their "learning curve" over the past 40 years has taken them through 4 major eras.

Before 1970

Before 1970, most businesses, including hospitality-related businesses, were doing nothing special about the environment, although a few leaders were beginning to wonder how their actions affected the environment, and a few manufacturing companies were beginning to make what they thought of as environmentally friendly products. Some very early pioneers in the "nature" and "adventure" travel industry were discovering that guests from the developed world would pay to visit out-of-the-way places in the developing world, even (or especially) if they had to sleep in thatched dwellings, ride in dugout canoes, fend off exotic wildlife and participate in village life. Divers and bird watchers, along with mountain climbers and cultural adventurers drove this niche market, but almost nobody thought of "the environment" or "the village" as other than "the main attraction."

The 1970s

During the 1970s many countries began to develop regulations that governed environmental planning and "media specific" emissions (such as to air and water). Most business owners, including hospitality related businesses, responded by trying to be "in compliance" with these rules and regulations. The USA and dozens of other countries developed environmental impact assessment (EIA), which required certain kinds of proposals to be evaluated for their environmental impacts before going ahead. Environmental advocacy groups grew or were launched, but even these were focused outward, on what other organizations should (or should not) be "doing to" the environment.

Hospitality industry leaders applied for and received the necessary permits for their facilities and operations; more ordinary vacationers and business travelers began to frequent the "exotic" locales "discovered" by the early adopters, and the global tourism industry began to take off in earnest.

The 1980s

In the 1980s, a few businesses, especially those in the chemical and manufacturing industries or that sold into international markets, strove to go "beyond compliance" by developing technologies and approaches that exceeded their government compliance requirements. As industry leaders, many of these companies increased their profits as a result of their environmental practices (that is, they saved money) and increased their market share and sold more goods (that is, they made money).

The hotel industry diversified, with major brands adding a variety of levels of service, expanding into smaller markets, and catering to the business traveler. "Eco" and "adventure" and "nature" and "cultural" tourism ventures expanded, but still, not much attention was paid to "the environment" or "the people." Some business owners in this industry began to seek out "best practices," mostly as they related to physical plant design and operations, and mostly for the purpose of cost-efficiency: a lot of old furnaces were replaced in the 1980s.

The 1990s

By the 1990s the idea of "eco-efficiency" was beginning to take hold: business owners realized that taking care of the environment was something that could benefit the enterprise. Books were written, software developed, and consultancies formed to nurture "strategic" environmental management systems to systematize and institutionalize specific steps that both ensured compliance and further improved a business's bottom line. The ISO 14000 family of international environmental management system standards was born as a follow-on to the ISO 9000 family of international quality standards, and more kinds of enterprises got into the game. Developing countries now had access to the playing field (whether or not it was quite level yet), and achieving certification in one form or another began to become important to vendors, whether of wire, milk, or hospitality.

Many hotels began certifying to the quality standards, and some of their managers became curious about the environmental standards. Hospitality industry associations created guidelines, checklists, certifications, videos, and "action packs" to spread the word about this new world of potential. But many industry observers also began writing "exposés" of industry failures: destruction of the environment by "eco" resorts, exploitation of the local populations by "cultural" tours, poor (or no) visitor management so the ruins were being further ruined, cruise ships dumping sewage inside harbors, and other widely-known horror stories. Some leading hospitality business owners sought out systems and processes that would ensure these horrors never happened to them.

The 2000s and beyond

In the 2000s and beyond, society and industry leaders have again raised the bar, striving for sustainability – not just compliance or eco-efficiency – through "design for environment" and life cycle analysis, the LEED building standards, and explicit mainstreaming of environmental goals. This entails changing organizational cultures to enhance environmental awareness and actions and – if it is done thoughtfully – will result in even more profits, streamlined processes, and social equity.

Hospitality-related organizations such as Green Globe, Green Seal, Oceans Blue, the Green Hotels Association, the Green Restaurant Association, the World Tourist Organization, The National Ski Areas Association, The International Ecotourism Society, Worldwide Fund for Animals, Conservation International and others have launched initiatives designed to inform, educate, and assist their members in developing fully sustainable businesses. Business owners now are talking about future visions, and strategies, and guiding principles.

Customers are beginning to drive sustainability through their purchasing patterns. Given the choice, they often will choose what they perceive to be the "more sustainable" product or service, at least in part because their children have extremely high levels of awareness and often influence their choices.

Past and Future Business Systems

Let's put his brief history into some context of overall business systems; the hospitality industry, after all, partakes of its surrounding culture, expectations, and foibles. Twentieth century business systems were extraordinarily wasteful. Experts estimate that up to 94 percent of all manufacturing output of these systems is "non-product" – i.e., waste – and that 80 percent of the actual "product" becomes waste within 6 months. Companies have been buffeted by both regulatory and market pressures; compliance with environmental regulations and with customer demands requires a constant rethinking of current practice and retooling of manufacturing facilities. An increasingly competitive marketplace also demands rethinking, to ensure that money is not wasted making "non-products" which have no value and do not contribute to long-term profits.

Companies that continue to bounce back and forth between regulatory and customer demands waste a lot of their management energy and financial resources *reacting* rather than *designing*, and they can simply forget about *leading* their industries. The management systems in common use can help companies improve their reactions, but don't provide much help for actually designing a sustainable company.

Business writers such as Paul Hawken, Ray Anderson, and Brian Natriss describe a quite different possibility for the future shape of commerce (see references at the end of this book). According to this vision, those future, sustainable, leading businesses will have eliminated "non-product" output through materials reductions, reuse, reclamation, recycling, or process redesign. They will have incorporated new energy sources, primarily renewables, and will have created much more value for their product. They will have benefited their community of workers, as well as the larger community of which they form a part. They will have protected and enhanced, not destroyed, their natural environment. The amount of flexibility and self-determination will have increased for these companies, and their bottom lines will have improved dramatically. Projects ranging from creating the "evergreen" commercial carpet leasing program from Interface, Inc. to the complete sustainability overhaul of the Skandic Hotel chain demonstrate the practicality of these new approaches, in terms of customer satisfaction, company profits, and industry leadership.

Wouldn't you like to have some of this?

The Triple Bottom Line

Leaders in the sustainability arena often talk of measuring performance on the "Triple Bottom Line," by which they mean *Planet,* or natural capital; *Profit,* or financial capital; and *People,* or human capital. John Elkington's 1999 book *Cannibals with Forks* contains an eloquent discussion of these concepts, with many examples.

An enterprise benefits itself when it produces measurable benefits to the Planet through environmental protection, restoration and enhancement, and avoids or reduces waste, production of toxic materials, destruction of environmental resources.

An enterprise also benefits when it contributes actively to more than merely its own financial Profit, but also creates and enhances its goodwill, reputation, and leadership.

And an enterprise benefits when it takes into account its effects on People, including its own staff, customers, suppliers and stockholders, along with other stakeholders such as members of the larger community and humankind in general.

These three components are often described as the three essential legs of a stool:

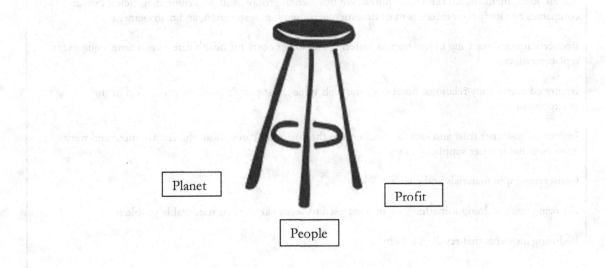

This "Triple Bottom Line" concept provides the basis of the sustainability approach we will take in this book: a basic question to keep on asking is "How will this activity support the my Planet, my Profit, and my People?"

Why Should You Care?

Only you, of course, can really answer that question.

But here are some of the things others who have entered the path toward sustainability have said motivated them (based on Blackburn, 2007; Kuhre, 1995; Tibor, 1996; and reviewers of early drafts of this book):

Assuring customers of commitment to demonstrable environmental management

Protection of the environment through reduction of hazardous and non-hazardous waste, resource conservation, and other global and local environmental issues

Making my business stronger and more competitive

Maintaining good public/community relations

Satisfying investor criteria and improving access to capital

Demonstrate regulatory compliance and improve agency/ industry relations

Reduce costs, especially in environmental control and remediation

Enhancing image and market share

Helping employees feel good about their work because they know they are doing something important about the environment

Strengthen risk management, compliance, productivity and credibility

Establish effective management systems, which are simply good business

Stakeholders, including investors, the public, environmental groups, and government agencies, expect companies to satisfy their interests in environmental protection, restoration, and management

Reduced injuries, resulting in less human suffering and lower costs for health care, down time, equipment replacement, etc.

Improved community relations, because of the high value most people place on protection of the environment

Improved customer trust and satisfaction, because the customer cares about the environment and wants assurance that his/her suppliers do too

Conserving input materials and energy

Knowing you are doing something about what used to seem like an insurmountable problem

Reducing incidents that result in liability

Improving cost control

Is there anything on this list that you *don't* want?

Remember, *compliance* with laws, regulations, permit requirements, etc. is the baseline: if you are not in compliance, you can't stay in business. *Sustainability* means moving far beyond mere compliance, to a way of doing business that serves you, your employees, your customers, the community at large, and future generations. In short, it is the business model for the 21st century.

The Basics of Sustainability

The three essential components of any sustainability program are practices, processes, and principles. We can use a familiar diagram to illustrate the role these three components play:

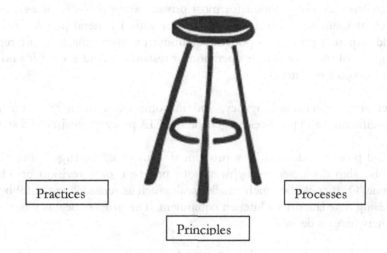

Practices

Principles

Processes

Practices

Using the hang tag that allows guests to choose whether or not to launder their linens is a good example of a very helpful practice, when it is carried out.

Good environmental, social and economic practices, the specific actions you and your staff take every day to provide your customers with the best products and services you know how, are essential to building a sustainable business.

Many businesses find it easiest to begin their journey toward sustainability here, because it is relatively easy to take small actions that change or enhance existing practices, and their results are relatively easy to measure:

- ❑ installing energy-efficient lighting,
- ❑ composting food wastes,
- ❑ recycling or reusing containers,
- ❑ applying kitchen grey water to landscape watering,
- ❑ providing benefits and incentives to employees,
- ❑ involving the local community in expansion planning,
- ❑ enlisting your customers for suggestions,
- ❑ instituting performance measures,
- ❑ laundering the linens less.

All are steps in the right direction, and you will want to continue to take these actions no matter how far along the path you wind up. Some organizations never get beyond a comprehensive list of practices – "this is what we do here" – and that's OK. If you routinely apply all the "best practice" ideas in the Green Hotels Association's 75 page compendium, for example, you will be doing very well indeed!

One way to approach the design of best practices is to conduct environmental impact assessment (EIA): prior to making a decision about a particular action that may affect the environment, the proponent determines what kinds of effects, beneficial or adverse, the action could have on the physical, social, or economic environment, then develops alternatives or tools to avoid or mitigate the adverse effects and to expand and enhance the beneficial effects.

In the US, such analyses are not required for most private sector projects, unless you operate in certain states (such as California) or on Federal land or with a Federal permit. But many other parts of the world require a project proponent to submit extensive checklists or reports on the environmental impacts of their hotel, tour operation or restaurant. And even if it's not required, it can be very helpful as you'll see later on.

Although each country, government agency, and in some cases industry sector may have a different set of specific rules and practices, in general the EIA process consists of 5 steps:

1. A proposed project is defined by a proponent. This could be large scale, such as a new hotel, cruise ship dock, access highway, tour program, or a revision or addition to an existing one. Or it could be much smaller scale, such as remodeling the lobby of a facility or purchasing new laundry or kitchen equipment. The process begins when one or more project alternatives is defined.

2. Impacts on the environment are identified, defined, studied, and debated for each alternative, including No Action. For large-scale projects, this step may be conducted by government agencies, private consultants, project proponents, or NGOs, depending on the specific rules governing the EIA process. For small-scale projects, the staff and management evaluate those aspects of the proposal that may impact the environment, for example by altering the energy usage of a facility. Sometimes the rules allow the public to have a say in this step, sometimes not.

3. An evaluation of the nature of the identified impacts takes place: are they significant or not? In some EIA processes government agencies or a government oversight entity (such as a Department of the Environment) makes or helps make this determination. In the US process, the determination is made by the government agency proposing to approve the project, in consultation with other agencies with jurisdiction over specific resources such as air, water, wildlife, or cultural heritage sites.

4. If impacts are serious but can be mitigated, mitigation is designed (and sometimes argued over or negotiated or litigated), put in place, and the project goes to Step 5. If impacts are not serious at all, usually the project goes directly to Step 5. Sometimes the impacts are so serious, or the project is so controversial environmentally that it may not take place at all.

5. Usually, however, the proponent proceeds with the project. This may involve preparing and circulating a document to the public (such as the US Environmental Impact Statement, or EIS), or submitting an application for permit approval. The point is that at some time, unless the project is cancelled, it usually will go forward (hopefully with appropriate mitigation measures in place).

So, it is possible to think of the EIA process as comprising what I call "The Five Big EIA Questions:"

1. What do we want to do?
2. What resources are affected?
3. How serious are the impacts?
4. How can we mitigate them, if needed?
5. When can we start the project?

The problem with EIA is that this process does not, by itself, help determine *what should be done*. Rather, it presupposes that you have a project in mind, and it enables you to determine what specific practices to undertake with respect to the environment – physical, social, or economic – to make it happen. That's OK, but EIA by itself only evaluates proposed practices, so it is just the first leg of the stool.

Processes

The second leg of the stool, and the next step along the path to sustainability is the development of processes that ensure your practices are applied correctly, do what they were intended to do, and are moving your enterprise in the desired direction. I mean by this, of course, that you need a management system for the environmental aspects of your enterprise. This "environmental management system" (EMS) is the "beyond compliance" phase of sustainability.

ISO 14001 and similar environmental management systems have become popular recently, and provide a valuable tool for organizing the previously separate functions of policy, program development, procedures, training, monitoring, continuous improvement, community involvement, pollution prevention, and environmental regulatory compliance into an integrated system. Companies now talk about "strategic" EMSs, or add "environment" into their ISO 9000 total quality management systems to create "TQEM" or total quality *environmental* management approaches. Again, all of these are steps in the right direction.

To continue the hang tag example, your policies about energy, water, detergent and housekeeping practices will define how and when the hang tags are used; your training program for housekeeping staff will teach them what to do when the tag is used; you will monitor and correct any mistakes; and you will review the results periodically to ensure you are getting the environmental, social, and economic effects you expected.

To implement a typical EMS, a business owner begins by conducting a situation review, which identifies baseline data about the environmental impacts and aspects of the enterprise. Next s/he develops an environmental policy, and puts together a program plan (including goals and objectives) to implement the policy and achieve the desired results. S/he conducts training, writes procedures, manages information, and define and accomplish other actions that help implement the policy and move toward the goals and objectives. Monitoring is conducted throughout the process, and corrective actions are taken when toxic or hazardous materials (such as fuel) are spilled, or other pollutants are released to the environment. A top management review is conducted to determine whether targets were met, and the cycle begins again. The system is focused on steering your enterprise in the "right direction:" the direction you choose. It is designed to facilitate continual improvement, over time, based on periodic measurements of progress.

Thus, it is possible to think of this process as comprising a set of "Five Big EMS Questions" as follows:

1. Where are we now, with respect to the physical, social or economic environment?
2. Where do we want to go?
3. How will we get there?
4. Are we getting there?
5. Is it still where we want to go?

Notice that there is still no way from within the EMS framework to determine *what should be done* or to align the EMS with a set of principles that will get you *beyond* "beyond compliance." Having a company environmental policy is an essential beginning for thinking about what should be done, but there still needs to be some meaningful yardstick against which the policy itself can be measured: how useful is it in guiding actions toward the desired goal? And what *is* a desirable kind of goal to have?

It is in fact possible that your policy may achieve certain desirable environmental goals but may undermine others. For example, a specific waste-reduction policy leading to a menu change could help a hotel reduce or eliminate waste on a per-serving basis from its food and beverage function, but cause it to increase its overall waste due to increased product sales as a result. An EMS by itself is only the second leg of the stool.

Principles

Neither EIA nor EMS activities, by themselves, provide tools to resolve argument or controversy about relatively small-scale environmental details. For example, much EIA litigation in the US focuses on disagreements among experts about the severity of projected environmental impacts: how serious is the loss of 10 acres of wetlands versus 12, or even 200? the loss of one endangered species over another? job creation versus environmental degradation? Likewise, an EMS by itself does not lift the discussion above how many parts per million of a pollutant are considered "dangerous," it merely provides a tool for ensuring that your operation never produces emissions that exceed the regulatory target.

 The metaphor of a tree with many leaves is useful to describe this phenomenon: the leaves represent the details, about which there can be many opinions, conflicting research data, or conflicting political or philosophical viewpoints. What is needed is to get beyond the leaves, so all parties can see and understand the underlying framework of trunk and branches and roots. The Natural Step (TNS) is one such current leading-edge sustainability framework that provides the basis for consensus and communication among the parties; it is the one I will use in this book. It constitutes the third leg of the stool.

First, a little history (again!). The Natural Step (TNS) began as a Swedish NGO, founded in 1989 by a medical doctor and cancer researcher, Karl-Henrik Robért. It now has a global reach, with companies adhering to the principles in major markets around the world. TNS companies as of this writing include worldwide giants such as IKEA, Interface, Inc. and Electrolux along with regional or local product and services providers such as Collins Pine, Placon Corporation (a plastic packaging company) and Skandic Hotels.

Based on the laws of physics (thermodynamics) and of natural systems, TNS provides a firm scientific basis for developing consensus around underlying principles that are "non-negotiable" *in nature*. That is, violation of any of four basic "system conditions" will violate basic laws of nature such that human society will become non-sustainable. Therefore, we humans must obey these laws of nature if we are to survive and sustain our societies, whatever our political, philosophical, or scientific opinions.

In addition, seeking to reverse damage done by the failure of previous generations to adhere to these laws can lead to developing the restorative economy Paul Hawken refers to in *The Ecology of Commerce*, cited above.

The four basic non-negotiable system conditions for organizations and for humans to survive – to be sustainable – are:

1. The organization must systematically decrease its dependence on materials extracted from the lithosphere (for example, fossil fuels, metals, minerals and other non-renewable materials from the earth's crust)

2. The organization must systematically decrease its dependence on persistent unnatural substances (for example, man-made chemicals that do not biodegrade because they are exotic to nature and so there are no natural mechanisms to degrade them)

3. The organization must systematically decrease its dependence on activities which encroach on productive parts of nature (for example, forests, rivers, wetlands, biodiversity – in other words, that harm the ecological systems that produce food, air, water necessary to human life)

4. The organization must systematically decrease its dependence on using large amounts of resources in relation to added human value (that is, that violate the basic principles of social equity).

An easy way to remember these four principles is what I call the "Four E's":

1. Extraction
2. Exotics
3. Ecology
4. Equity

An organization should avoid the first two (extraction and exotics) and protect and enhance the second two (ecology and equity).

> ## *The extent to which an organization succeeds in this is the extent to which it is on the path toward sustainability.*

So for any project, program or decision, the "Five Big TNS Questions" are:

1. How does this project affect extraction? (that is, can it be done in a way that materials are not extracted faster than they are replaced, or the use of non-renewables is minimized?)

2. How does it affect exotics? (that is, can the use of exotics – mostly chemicals – be reduced or eliminated?)

3. How does it affect the ecology? (that is, can it be done in a way that preserves or restores the productive natural environment, including water, soil, air, flora and fauna?)

4. How does it affect equity? (that is, can it be done so that one group of people does not preclude opportunity for others?)

5. Should we do it at all? (that is, can we achieve the desired end result in a sustainable way?)

Note that this framework of sustainability "system conditions" automatically provides a *direction* to planning not offered by either EIA or EMS by themselves because it occurs at a higher logical level. Discussions take place about the trunk and the branches and the roots of the tree, not about the leaves. This shift in perspective automatically leads to asking the most important question of all, *should we do this project – here, now, in this way – at all?* For example, if your chosen direction is away from extraction, and your proposed new hotel expansion as currently designed requires vast amounts of virgin and non-recyclable raw materials from the lithosphere for construction (such as stone or stainless steel), you can easily understand that this project will not contribute to sustainability either of your enterprise or of the planet (including human society). And you can decide to do it differently, or not at all.

In the hang tag example, by applying the system principles you might choose to have an introductory briefing (perhaps at a social hour) for incoming guests rather than purchase a hang tag, or to provide a clearly marked (and locally made) basket for soiled linens in each room, or to simply state that linens are washed every other day – period – or, or, or.... Suddenly lots of options present themselves, any of which will move you along the path, and you can determine the costs and benefits of each one against the others.

Thus the role of TNS is as an integrator of EIA and EMS into a broader and more effective framework. If your goal is economic and environmental sustainability, EIA becomes a tool for exploring environmental impacts caused by the organization's projects, activities and programs; it focuses on the leaves of the tree. EMS is the tool for systematizing internal processes to minimize such impacts; it focuses on connecting the leaves to the branches. TNS is the framework, the actual trunk and branches and roots of the tree, without which both other tools are directionless. It forces us to think outside the box and to generate lasting solutions rather than giving a Band-Aid to a patient who should be having triple by-pass surgery.

Put another way, TNS provides the compass, the direction toward sustainability, while your EMS is the ship that carries you there, and your EIA practices are the crew.

You can have a beautiful cruise ship and a highly skilled captain and crew, but unless you have a tool to set the appropriate direction you will sail the seas forever and never reach a destination worth going to.

The rest of this book will walk you through the practices, processes and principles you need to put (or keep) your hotel, ship, tour, or other hospitality-related facility on the path to sustainability – *forever!*

Chapter 3 - Sustainability Practices

 Good practices are essential components of a successful sustainability program. This chapter will provide you with some sample checklists and tools for creating your own lists of good practices, and protocols for determining which ones to implement first and which ones will move you farthest down the path toward your desired future. Figures 3.1-3.23 (pp. 28-31) illustrate some popular practices in use around the world today.

Practices involve *actions* – "this is what we do" – and often *things* – "this is the kind of (light bulb, detergent, laundry bag, toilet, compost bin) we do it with." Changing existing practices requires money to buy the things, and training programs to teach the staff to carry out the actions. If you buy the things but fail to train the staff to use them, you are wasting your money, or worse (remember the hang tag story?)

Reasons for adopting "green" practices often include:

- ❑ Saving money (on energy, water, waste disposal)
- ❑ Keeping up with the competition (everyone is doing it)
- ❑ Meeting customer demand (via comments on the comment form)
- ❑ Meeting regulator requirements (water treatment and use standards)
- ❑ Achieving "green" certification (building construction, meeting practices)
- ❑ Doing the right thing

Let me say right now that you *can* have it all: you can achieve all these goals and more. But – and it is a very big but – you can't do it all at once, and you must coordinate your efforts or you will be right back into the hang tag quagmire.

Here's why: to accomplish these goals, the purchasing manager needs to save money; the advertising manager needs to keep up with the competition (and surpass them if possible); the marketing manager needs to respond to the customers; the environmental manager needs to meet regulatory requirements; company headquarters needs certificates to frame; and the recent environmental sciences graduate working the front desk needs to do the right thing.

So let's say they each come up with a way to meet their needs: the purchasing manager buys cheaper detergent; the advertising manager prints up beautiful brochures touting the natural wonders of the environment; the marketing manager buys softer pillows; the environmental manager buys low flow toilets; and the front desk clerk convinces the housekeeping manager to switch to low-wattage light bulbs in the guest rooms. So far so good, right?

But.

I see lots of money going out, lots of good efforts being made, and *lots of potential for disaster.* What if the detergent requires hot water to work effectively? What if the brochures are printed on glossy, non-recyclable paper with toxic ink? What if the new pillows contain a volatile gas that some guests are allergic to? What if the new toilets must be flushed twice each time because the existing plumbing was not designed for them? And what if the old light bulbs are dumped all at once into a local landfill and the higher-wattage lamps in the lobby are not replaced? How did all the potential savings, and the increased customer satisfaction, and the good feelings from doing the right thing vanish so quickly?

You didn't reach your goals because you didn't go about the process of adopting your new practices *systematically*. You just found one you liked, adopted it, and went on about your business. And then another one. And another one. And another one.

You wouldn't do that if you adopted a child, would you? Of course not! You'd invest a lot of time with your current family figuring out whether to do it at all, and if the answer was yes, what kind of child to adopt: an infant or an older child, perhaps? You might also consider its country of origin, or its gender, or whether you are willing to adopt one with special challenges or with siblings. You would analyze the costs for its entire life: clothing, schooling, toys and medical expenses. Only then you would bring the child home and begin the process of integrating it into your everyday life. You would teach it, day by day, what it needs to know: how to speak, how to behave, how to eat. You would pay attention to its progress, and to whether or not things were generally working out in the way you expected. You would tell everyone you know about the new addition to the family, and enlist their support and help in raising it. You probably would not adopt another one until the first one was well integrated, and you were confident things were working out.

That is exactly the process you need to go through when you adopt a new sustainability practice.

Once you realize that a change in one aspect will often have repercussions in many others, it will be easier to choose a specific practice that will be beneficial for several aspects of the enterprise. For example, instead of buying new, more energy-efficient air conditioners, why not plant trees to shade the building during the hottest part of the day? The investment is about the same and trees require no ongoing electricity (although they do require water and maintenance). By choosing native species you can help restore the habitat and encourage wildlife for guests to experience. You can provide ongoing jobs for local people caring for the landscape, and avoid extracting more non-renewable metals from the earth to manufacture unnecessary air conditioners.

But you would never notice these interactions if you considered only the HVAC system and sought only to lower electricity usage. Nor would you have the benefit of involving the groundskeepers in the discussion, or the opportunity to enhance the beauty of your facility, or the pleasure of giving your guests something to do besides eat and run to the nearest off-site attraction!

So enough theory. Let's move on to the "how to" part.

How to Choose Appropriate Sustainability Practices

This part of the book will walk you through some activities designed to help you systematically identify and evaluate potential areas in which you might choose to adopt new sustainability practices. If you have already adopted some, fine; you can evaluate their effectiveness and decide whether to keep them, or seek out other ways to accomplish the same goal. Remember, you are in charge, and you don't have to do everything all at once.

To develop a systematic way of going about adopting sustainability practices involves nothing more than a pencil and paper (remember my Principle #1: "Keep it sweet and simple"): you are going to create a checklist for your facility that takes into account all the aspects of your operations that interact with your physical, social, and economic environment.

Step 1 – Brainstorm the Operations

Get out some paper and a pencil, and begin by thinking about all the different functions, activities, buildings, systems, people, departments, materials, suppliers, facilities, utilities, and *stuff* that makes up your operation. This is a brainstorming activity; the more people you can involve in this step, the better. Make sure you involve people who actually do the work: the chef, the groundskeeper, the sailor, the driver, the housekeeper, the front desk clerk.

You might structure the activity as a series of questions:

- ❑ What is it that you do? (run a hotel, feed business travelers, operate a cruise line, lead camping tours in the outback, make people happy, provide jobs for local people, conduct efficient operations, generate repeat customers, receive industry awards)

- ❑ Where do you do it? (in an urban setting, on a jungle island, in the Caribbean, 500 kilometers from anywhere; in the tropics, in the mountains, at the beach, in the desert)

- ❑ How do you do it? (in a single large building, on an open patio, on 75-year-old sailing ships, with 4-wheel-drive buses, with a crew of 5, using gas-powered lawnmowers)

- ❑ What do you need to do it with? (electricity, water, perishable foodstuffs, plastic wrap, metal containers, table settings, wind, fuel, paper, computers, a tennis court, life rafts, parking, cooperation from the village, permission from the government)

- ❑ When do you do it? (summer, winter, all year long, only in the evening)

- ❑ Who does it with you? (staff, customers, suppliers, contractors, villagers, government regulators)

Write down the answers. Don't worry about ordering them; remember, this is brainstorming, so any input is OK, and in fact the more you get the easier it will be later.

An easy way to do this is to provide each participant with a pad of sticky notes and a pencil; have them write their ideas, one to a note, then stick them up on flip chart or butcher paper for everyone to see. You could even decide to color-code them in some way. Later the ideas can easily be organized and re-organized as desired.

Step 2 – Sort the List into Categories

Now sort the big list you have into manageable categories. One way to do this is to divide up your operation into various relevant components, as illustrated in the examples below. Here is where the sticky notes really come in handy!

Example 1

Here is how David Stipanuk and Harold Roffman divide up the world in their 2006 book, *Hospitality Facilities Management and Design*:

- ❑ Facility Systems
    - o Water and Wastewater Systems
    - o Electrical Systems
    - o Heating, Ventilating and Air Conditioning Systems

- o Lighting Systems
- o Laundry Systems
- o Telecommunications Systems
- o Safety and Security Systems
- o Waste Management
- o Food Service Equipment
- o Energy Management

- ❑ The Outer Envelope
    - o The Building and Exterior Facilities
    - o Parking Areas
- ❑ Facility Design
    - o Lodging Planning and Design
    - o Food Service Planning and Design
    - o Renovation

Example 2

In 1996, The American Hotel & Motel Association (AHMA), in cooperation with The International Hotel Association (IHA), The International Hotels Environment Initiative (IHEI) and the United Nations Environment Program (UNEP) produced a checklist booklet with a training video they called "The Environmental Action Pack for Hotels."

The booklet contains a "Green Health Check" based on a series of checklists that cover the following topics:

- ❑ Energy
- ❑ Solid Waste
- ❑ Water
- ❑ Effluents and Emissions
- ❑ Purchasing
- ❑ Business Issues

Each checklist contains questions to be answered "yes" or "no," such as "Have targets for reducing energy consumption been set?" and "Do you buy recycled or recyclable products where possible?" Each topic is given a score (based on the number of "yes" answers to the questions on the checklist), and each topic is given a priority ranking based on how low its score is: the lower the score, the higher the priority for improvement.

Sample "action checklists" also are provided for several departments:

- ❑ Housekeeping Staff
- ❑ Food and Beverage Staff
- ❑ Maintenance Staff
- ❑ Administration and Front Desk Staff

These provide a space to list goals/objectives, and a space to list specific tasks to do or accomplishments during the measurement period.

Example 3

Green Seal's 1996 publication, *Greening Your Property*, organizes things a little differently, and adds some topics not covered before:

- ❑ Manage Energy Consumption
- ❑ Choose Efficient Lighting
- ❑ Manage Water Use
- ❑ Improve Indoor Air Quality
- ❑ Green Your Amenities and Services
- ❑ Publicize Your Program

The booklet also contains sample audit forms; worksheets for energy, lighting, and water;. and lists of suppliers of environmentally-friendly products (everything from bicycle racks to windows).

Example 4

Finally, the Green Hotel Association produces a compendium for its members, containing 75 pages of environmentally-friendly practices, suppliers, organizations, and tools, organized around the following topics:

- ❑ Employees
- ❑ Guest Rooms
- ❑ Chemically-sensitive Guests
- ❑ Public Areas
- ❑ Lawn and Garden
- ❑ Restaurants / Dining Areas / Bars
- ❑ Laundry
- ❑ Swimming Pool
- ❑ Solid Waste
- ❑ Recycling
- ❑ Waste Water
- ❑ Clean Air
- ❑ Noise Control
- ❑ Offices
- ❑ Marketing
- ❑ Purchasing
- ❑ Maintenance
- ❑ Conventions / Meetings
- ❑ New Construction / Refurbishing
- ❑ Community
- ❑ Government / Other Organizations
- ❑ Ecotourism

By now you are probably thinking these examples are overkill: "just tell me how to do it!" OK, here are some categories I have used with clients in the past:

- ❑ Functions: housekeeping, food and beverage, landscape, maintenance, guest services

- ❑ Facility systems: electrical, lighting, laundry, water and wastewater, HVAC, security, energy, solid waste, communications, physical plant

- ❑ Building(s) and associated features: walls, windows, doors, floors, roof, landscaping, parking, drainage, building design and siting

- ❑ People: customers, staff, suppliers, neighbors, regulators, travel agents

And on page 22 is a copy of a simple worksheet ("The Hospitality Forever™ Overview") that will help you get a "quick and dirty" sense of how well you are doing in the various areas of interest. It might be interesting to give one to each staff member (and customer?) and compare the answers you get. Feel free to customize it; I know you will anyway.

The objective here is to figure out in what categories you need to look for aspects of your enterprise that impact the environment. These will be the problems to be solved, and will suggest what kinds of new practices to explore. If you are already doing "well" in a particular category, however you define that, it will probably be more useful to begin with a category in which you are *not* already doing well (remember my Principle #2, "if it ain't broke, don't fix it").

The Hospitality Forever™ Overview

☐ **Housekeeping**
    1   2   3   4   5   6   7   8   9   10

☐ **Front Office**
    1   2   3   4   5   6   7   8   9   10

☐ **Landscaping**
    1   2   3   4   5   6   7   8   9   10

☐ **Food and beverage**
    1   2   3   4   5   6   7   8   9   10

☐ **Water, energy, chemical usage**
    1   2   3   4   5   6   7   8   9   10

☐ **Emissions and effluents**
    1   2   3   4   5   6   7   8   9   10

☐ **Purchasing**
    1   2   3   4   5   6   7   8   9   10

☐ **Customer satisfaction**
    1   2   3   4   5   6   7   8   9   10

☐ **Staff awareness**
    1   2   3   4   5   6   7   8   9   10

☐ **Regulatory situation**
    1   2   3   4   5   6   7   8   9   10

☐ **Income and investment**
    1   2   3   4   5   6   7   8   9   10

☐ **Business leadership**
    1   2   3   4   5   6   7   8   9   10

Step 3 – Identify Aspects and Impacts

Now that you have listed the who, what, where, when, and how, it's time to get specific about the aspects of those activities or facilities or systems that actually could or do have an impact on the environment. What does this mean?

An <u>aspect</u> can be defined as *an element of an organization's activities, products, or services that can interact with the environment.* So, food service clearly is an aspect of the hospitality business, but so is fuel storage on site, if that is where you store it.

An <u>impact</u> can be defined as *any change to the environment, whether adverse or beneficial, wholly or partially resulting from an organization's activities, products, or services.* So, while discharge of untreated wastewater into the lake (or the ocean) may be an output from an activity of your resort or cruise ship, the actual environmental impact is the unpleasant consequences for the water, the fish and all who depend on them.

You should put together a simple form on which to collect the data, like this:

Category:		
Subcategory:		
Date:	Completed by:	
Activity	**Environmental Aspects**	**Environmental Impacts**

Part of a completed form for the Housekeeping function might look like this:

Category: Housekeeping		
Subcategory: Cleaning Guest Rooms		
Date:	Completed by:	
Activity	**Environmental Aspects**	**Environmental Impacts**
Cleaning toilets	Use of cleansers and solvents	Pollution of ground, water, air
Floor polishing	Use of wax and solvents	Pollution of air, ground, water
Tidying room	Disposing of trash	Pollution of ground, water
Lighting the work area	Using electricity	Depletion of non-renewables
Etc.		

This is a very simple, preliminary analysis. At some point later on you might want to get more detailed, either about the specific activities, their aspects, or their impacts. But right now you are just beginning to learn how everything is connected to everything else.

If you change the cleanser used in the guest rooms, could the kitchen use some of the new type also? Why would you purchase energy-efficient washing machines, but keep using inefficient vacuum cleaners? Are there some floors you could sweep or mop instead of vacuuming? Are there floor materials that are easier to care for, and made of renewable materials too? If you change toilet chemicals how does that affect the septic system? If you provide glass carafes for water instead of plastic bottles, how does that affect your costs short- and long-term, and the environment?

You can see how this works, can't you?

This kind of analysis will lead you to ask such questions, which will lead you to adopt better – less wasteful, less polluting, less expensive, less complicated, more sustainable – practices.

Step 4 – Prioritize the Problems

Now you are going to begin prioritizing the problems. Marilyn R. Block in her 1999 book, *Identifying Environmental Aspects and Impacts*, lists 9 different scales on which to evaluate problems you identify during Step 3, as follows:

Severity Scale:	Likelihood Scale:	Frequency Scale:
1. Harmless 2. Mild 3. Moderate 4. Serious 5. Severe/catastrophic	1. Remote (<10%) 2. Low (11-33%) 3. Moderate (34-67%) 4. Likely (68-89%) 5. Very likely (> 90%)	1. Seldom (<2x/year) 2. Intermittent (1x/qtr) 3. Regular (monthly) 4. Repeated(1-2x/week) 5. Continuous (3x/week)
Boundaries Scale:	Controllability Scale:	Regulatory Status Scale:
1. Isolated 2. Confined 3. Local 4. Regional 5. Global	1. Directly controllable 2. Indirectly controllable 3. Influenceable 4. Indirectly influenceable 5. Uncontrollable	1. Unregulated 2. Company practice 3. Company policy 4. Regulated in future 5. Government regulated
Reportability Scale:	Stakeholder Concerns Scale:	Duration Scale:
1. Not reportable 2. Facility reports 3. Company reports 4. Corporate reports 5. Government reports	1. No concerns 2. Secondary for some 3. Secondary for all 4. Primary for some 5. Primary for all	1. Less than three months 2. Three-twelve months 3. One to three years 4. Three years or more 5. Irreversible

Some of these scales may be less relevant on a day-to-day basis than others, but you may generate strong stakeholder concerns about wastewater disposal, for example, even in the absence of specific government regulation of some hospitality functions (as some cruise lines have discovered the hard way).

You also may want to define some of the factors differently than Block did; that's OK too, as long as all the raters know what the terms mean in an explicit and reproducible way.

Now you have a tool for setting priorities: you have identified the aspects of your enterprise that can impact the environment; the nature of that impact; its severity, likelihood, frequency, controllability, duration; its relationship to stakeholder concerns; and any regulatory or reporting requirements.

Putting all this together, we might have the following table (yours may have more columns):

Aspect	Impact	Regulated	Duration	Frequency	Rank (see below)
Use of solvents	Water pollution	4	3	5	60
Use of solvents	Air emissions	5	1	5	25
(etc.)					

Notice that the *rank* is not the sum of the ratings, but their <u>product</u>; that is, you multiply all of the rating numbers together to come up with the overall ranking of each impact. This is because most of these characteristics are not related to each other, but each is simply a factor to be considered. If the characteristics were related, you would add them up. If you haven't studied your statistics for a while (or ever), just know that there is a good reason for this, or else just trust me: it will make your life easier.

Step 5 – Pull It All Together

At long last you are ready to put it all together. Remember my Principle #3: "Your people are your most important resource."

Step 5 is a group project.

Make sure everyone who conducts an activity that has an aspect that has an impact gets input into this process. They are the ones who will have to do whatever it is that gets chosen for the new practices; they are the ones who can come up with the ideas for changes that may not even involve purchasing expensive equipment....

Let's go back to the famous (or infamous) hang tag for a moment. Mostly what it seems to do is make money for the companies that print and distribute hang tags. What are some of the problems that you are trying to solve with the hang tag?

Problem #1: Wasting energy in the laundry

Possible solutions:
- purchase more energy efficient laundry equipment
- only wash linens every third day for continuing guests
- offset with energy efficiencies in other functions
- develop on-site wind, wave, or solar energy sources

Problem #2: Wasting water in the laundry

Possible solutions:
- purchase more water efficient laundry equipment
- only wash linens every third day for continuing guests
- offset with water efficiencies in other functions
- re-use grey water from laundry for landscape watering

Problem #3: Wanting to demonstrate your "green" credentials

Possible solutions:
- Achieve and post a recognized "green" certificate in the lobby
- Tell customers about your "green" practices
- Provide a "green" credit on the guest's bill
- Use a hang tag, and *do what you promise*

So this step simply involves presenting the problems and asking for suggestions for solutions.

Once you begin to identify the actual nature of the problem to be solved, you (or someone at your facility) can come up with lots of suggestions for ways to solve it. Those solutions, when they are identified, thought out, compared, evaluated, and wisely (and completely) adopted, *are your new sustainable practices*.

Step 6 – Adopt and Follow Through

You are finished with this part.

Oh, occasionally you might need to find sources of "environmentally friendly" cleaning products, or recycled office paper, or composting equipment, or low-flow shower heads, or solar panels, or low-wattage lighting. That's what the Internet is for, to help you find *things*.

But YOU need to figure out what problems to solve, and in what sequence. That is, you need to define the *actions* that constitute the actual practices: "we do it this way here." Then train the staff, measure the progress, fix anything that doesn't work the way you expected it to, and move on to the next problem.

Shortcut to Sustainable Practices

Here's a secret that will jump start your program: do one thing at a time. You may lose some synergy among the various departments and functions, and you may discover some time in the future that you could have been achieving even more if both the laundry and the kitchen had collaborated on finding suitable cleaning agents. But if you do these 6 steps for one particular function, facility, operational area, system or process, you will be on the path, and you can always add companions as you continue the journey.

And please don't just pick a new practice because you saw some sexy equipment in a catalogue, or because your competitor is doing it, or because someone (even a consultant!) suggested it. Do enough analysis, with pencil and paper and your capable staff, to figure out what needs fixing; then use the same tools to develop approaches that actually fix the problem rather than cause new ones.

Remember, most practices involve *actions* (what you do) plus *things* (what you do it with). Things (equipment, supplies, materials) cost money, require maintenance, and require replacement when the technology changes (as it will). Actions are relatively cheap, easy to do, and easy to change.

For example, you *could* purchase energy-efficient lighting for every area at your facility, or you could simply turn off the lights when you are not using them. You *could* replace all the air conditioners with more efficient models, or simply plant some trees and open the windows. You *could* purchase more energy-efficient leaf blower equipment, or just hire someone to sweep the walks daily.

Don't jump too fast at technology solutions! Only by comparing the actual costs and benefits of these practices can you decide among them. And remember, at the beginning, you are just beginning: make sure the baby steps you take now will provide a firm footing for your later journey toward a full-fledged sustainability program.

For example, consider the recent technology trends with regard to the Internet. At the turn of the 21st century, many major hotels invested thousands of dollars wiring their facilities with Ethernet cables to provide in-room Internet access to business customers; they often passed this cost on to their customers by charging a daily fee for using the connection. On the other hand, most smaller hotels (including some of the lower-cost brands owned by the majors) provided a "business center" where guests could use the hotel's equipment for free. When wi-fi technology came along, these smaller facilities simply bought a few $100 routers and offered free in-room Internet access – presto, no wires to install, maintain, or remove – while their major cousins were still charging their daily fee.

The fee may make the facility a bit more money at first but it is a real irritant for business travelers, who can simply go to the coffee shop (or a lower-cost hotel) next door and log on for free. And who wants grumpy customers who can't get the quality of service they expect from you without paying extra? (Can you guess that I am one of those grumpy customers?)

One small action that any of these facilities could have taken to make the business traveler's life easier would have been to create a business center with carrels in which the guests could hook up their laptops to the hotel's Ethernet system. There would have been no need to wire the entire facility, ever, or to charge a fee. And when wi-fi came along, the business center would still be there (for people who like to get out of their rooms once in a while) and the $100 routers could simply be added to the system.

So sometimes by waiting a bit, by being a little behind the curve, a different, more effective and less costly solution will present itself.

Short List of Sustainable Practices

Here it is! The official cheat sheet of sustainable hospitality practices, culled from experience, publications, the Internet – and tested throughout the world.

I have saved this for last because the biggest problem with practices is that people adopt them and then think they have therefore accomplished something important. Adopting any particular practice is just the first step in your journey toward sustainability, and it has to be done with care and thought. If you have gone through the steps outlined above, and really considered and prioritized the problems you are trying to solve, you are now ready for the list below.

Category	Sustainability Practices
Energy	Purchase efficient lighting (see Plate 1) Purchase dimmers Purchase automatic room light switch sensors Purchase key tags for guest rooms (see Plate 1) Turn lights off when not using them Install skylights and clerestory windows Purchase efficient laundry equipment Launder guest linens only every 3rd day for continuing guests Line-dry articles if climate permits Wash in cold water Purchase efficient HVAC equipment Retain or plant trees to shade buildings Install windows that open and provide cross-ventilation Install awnings to shade windows Use siting design to maximize winter heat and minimize summer heat Purchase on-site renewable power equipment (solar, wind, wave) Bake with full ovens to minimize fuel consumption

Water	Monitor and fix leaks immediately
	Install low flow fixtures throughout (not only in guest rooms!)
	Provide appropriate signage (see Plate 1)
	Purchase efficient equipment for laundry, landscape, maintenance
	Water landscape early in the day to conserve moisture
	Use drip systems rather than overhead sprays to water landscape
	Use kitchen grey water for landscape
	Turn off water when not being used
	Purchase "instant" hot water heaters (but check on energy costs!)
Air Quality	Avoid use of volatile chemicals for cleaning, painting, maintenance
	Use unscented detergents, softeners, candles
	Filter air if needed (dust, smog, smoke)
	Designate an area outdoors for tobacco smoking
	Avoid pressed-wood products containing urea (formaldehyde)
	Use carpet certified as low-emission by the Carpet and Rug Institute
	Ventilate all public and guest spaces with outside air (if quality permits)
	Clean up spills, water leaks, etc. on carpet immediately
	Use low VOC paints, coatings, thinners
Landscape	Use native plants in landscape design (they know how to grow here!)
	Use kitchen grey water for watering
	Compost kitchen waste and apply to plantings
	If you must have a lawn, use grass species that require little or no water
	Have frequent guests plant a tree, with a plaque with their name on it
	Create a walking garden (with labels) as an amenity
	Design a vegetated swale to handle roof and parking lot runoff
	Consider adding a "green" roof (it will save energy too)
	Plant herbs for use in the kitchen (a traditional "kitchen garden")

Examples of Sustainability Practices

Figure 3.1. Guest information on how to conserve.

Figure 3.2. A locally-made basket for soiled towels.

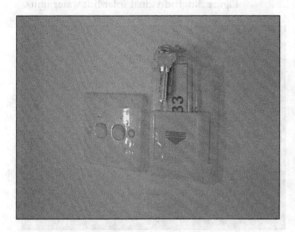

Figure 3.3. Key tag in place; the room power is on.

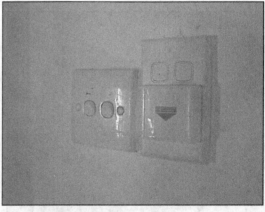

Figure 3.4. Key tag removed; the room power is off.

Figure 3.5. Locally-made clay bowls hold condiments.

Figure 3.6. Composting is useful and educational.

Figure 3.7. Dual-flow toilet in guest room.

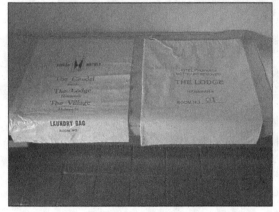

Figure 3.8. Individual solar hot water units.

Figure 3.9. Energy-efficient porch light on chalets.

Figure 3.10. Reusable cloth laundry bag on right.

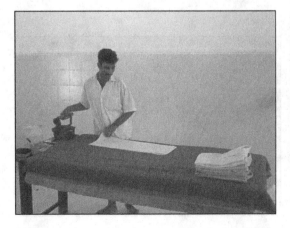

Figure 3.11. Charcoal irons burn waste coconut shells.

Figure 3.12. Grey water used for vegetable garden.

Figure 3.13. Use local flowers to decorate the bed.

Figure 3.14. Use retained native vegetation for shade.

Figure 3.15. Energy-efficient laundry facilities.

Figure 3.16. Grow your own food if you have space.

Figure 3.17. Reusable covers keep insects away.

Figure 3.18. Kitchen wastes feed pigs on the farm.

Sustainability Practices

Figure 3.19. Traditional architecture as meeting space.　Figure 3.20. Retain native vegetation on grounds.

Figure 3.21. Local villagers can guide tours. materials.　Figure 3.22. Guest information made of local

Figure 3.23. Some operations must be completely self-contained. Carrying your water minimizes plastic bottles.

Chapter 4 - Sustainability Processes

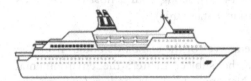 This is the next step along your sustainability path: developing a systematic approach to all of your practices, and pulling together a policy that moves you beyond mere "compliance."

Once you have the policy, of course, you will have to make sure you carry it out (remember the hang tag?), train the staff, measure progress, correct problems, tell your customers, and review everything periodically. But if you take it step by step, the process is really pretty straightforward. Ready to begin?

But of course, you have already begun: the first step to creating an environmental management system is the Situation Review. You have already accomplished that by going through the steps outlined in the Sustainability Practices chapter: you know what aspects of your operation may impact the environment, what regulations and other legal requirements apply, and how well you are doing. You probably have already adopted a few practices, and you may have some monitoring data that measure your progress so far.

The system you will be developing is based on the international ISO 14001 environmental management system standard. I use this approach for all my environmental management system projects, for three reasons:

1. It is international in scope. Whether you are in Stockholm or Sydney, Chicago or Colombo, the same standard applies. Notice I am not talking about *environmental* standards, such as for water quality (those will vary from place to place), but about *environmental management system* standards, which are uniform around the world.

2. Whether or not you ever choose to become certified under the standard (which involves an audit by an qualified third party and certification by an accredited organization), you can feel confident that your system meets the most recognized international criteria.

3. If you do choose to become certified in the future, your efforts will not have been wasted, and you will have all the parts in place for a successful third-party certification audit.

Here is how Joseph Cascio, in his 1999 *ISO 14000 Handbook* describes the standard. ISO 14000:

- is a framework for managing significant environmental aspects you can control and over which you can be expected to have an influence;
- is for use by any company, any size, anywhere in the world;
- is a voluntary consensus, private-sector standard;
- is systems-based, placing reliance on the system, not on individual specialists;
- represents a paradigm shift toward holistic management and total employee involvement;
- represents a shift to proactive thinking and acting
- urges employees to define their roles from the bottom up and requires top management backing, resources and visibility to support them.

First, a little history (again!). ISO stands for International Organization for Standardization;

headquartered in Geneva, Switzerland, it is a worldwide federation of national standards bodies. Currently 118 countries are represented in ISO. ISO 14001 is part of a <u>family</u> of environmental standards, called ISO 14000. Within this family, there are standards for the environmental management system itself (ISO 14001 and 14004); environmental auditing (ISO 14010, 14011, 14012); and environmental performance evaluation (ISO 14031), along with a host of standards related to products (labeling, life cycle assessment, and product standards).

The international ISO standards are developed by representatives of the standards bodies from the various countries, though a Technical Committee for the subject matter; the environmental management system technical committee is TC 207. National standards bodies (such as the American National Standards Institute – ANSI – in the US) may create Technical Advisory Groups, or TAGs, to assist them in this work.

I served as a member of the US TAG to TC 207 in the late 1990s, during development and testing of the first version of the ISO 14001 standard. The standard was slightly revised in 2004; that is the version used in this book.

Whew. If you really want more detail on all this, go to http://www.iso.org.ch and plow around there.

The Five Big EMS Questions

If you were to look at the actual ISO 14001 standard, you would notice that it has 17 sections, divided into 5 categories: Policy, Planning, Implementation and Operation, Checking, and Management Review. (You can't look at the complete text here, because no one but ISO is allowed to publish the entire text. But don't worry, I will show you *lots* of excerpts from the relevant sections as we come to them.)

This sequence of actions is often diagramed as an endless circle, like this:

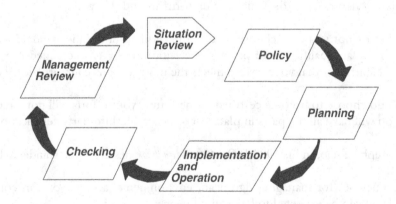

Figure 4.1. The "standard" EMS diagram.

Notice I have put a kind of "pre" step in, before Policy: Situation Review. You have done much of this already, during the Practices activities. Why is this included?

Suppose you didn't have an environmental policy, and I came in to your enterprise one day and asked you create one on the spot. What would you do? Where would you start? What should you include? Should you offer to comply with environmental requirements? Should you use the word "protect"? Would you ask any of your staff to help, or just make something up? What would you base these promises and goals – because that's what a policy represents, promises and goals – on, in the real world?

That's what a lot of consultants, and people of good will who are working through developing an environmental management system on their own, try to do: they try to start with the policy. That is crazy!

You can't develop an environmental policy from thin air!

That's why Anton Camarota and I developed the Five Big EMS Questions, which give you a logical framework within which to create your system:

1. Where are we now, with respect to the environment?
2. Where do we want to go?
3. How will we get there?
4. Are we getting there?
5. Is it still where we want to go?

Here is where they fit in the "standard" EMS diagram:

Figure 4.2. The Five Big EMS Questions related to the EMS "standard" diagram.

You have to begin with "Where are we now?" because you can't get from "here" to "there" unless you know where "here" is! In fact, "here" is the *only thing* you can ever really know, because "there" is just an idea, a goal, a dream. So every planning process must begin with an understanding of the current situation, which defines your starting point.

I have organized the other detailed steps a bit differently from how they are expressed in the standard, too, as you will notice if you pay close attention to the numbering of the sections of the standard in the excerpts below. Again, it's because the steps in this book are in the logical sequence of *how you will do them*, rather than in the same order they appear in the standard. You have to do them all anyway, to create a complete environmental management system, so you might as well do them in some logical order.

The rest of this chapter will walk you through the steps in developing and implementing an environmental management system that conforms to the ISO 14001 international standard.

Let's begin.

Question 1: Where Are We Now?

Situation Review

This is where you review the environmental aspects and impacts of your enterprise, whether it is a hotel, resort, cruise ship, tour operation, restaurant, bar, coffee shop, bistro, bed-and-breakfast inn, youth hostel, or dive shop. You have done a lot of this already, but now that work should be reviewed, polished, and written down formally.

Here are some things you might explore during this step (from ISO 14004 EMS Guidance):

---

a) identification of environmental aspects, including those associated with normal operating conditions, abnormal conditions including start-up and shut-down, and emergency situations and accidents;
b) identification of applicable legal requirements and other requirements to which the organization subscribes;
c) examination of existing environmental management practices and procedures, including those associated with procurement and contracting activities;
d) evaluation of previous emergency situations and accidents.

The review can also include additional considerations, such as
—an evaluation of performance compared with applicable internal criteria, external standards, regulations, codes of practice and sets of principles and guidelines,
—opportunities for competitive advantage, including cost reduction opportunities,
—the views of interested parties, and
—other organizational systems that can enable or impede environmental performance.

Think of this step as an opportunity to really take a look at the whole operation from the ground up (or, if you lead spelunking or skydiving tours, from even farther than that).

You will begin with identifying and evaluating environmental aspects and impacts, then pulling together all the legal and other requirements that apply to your enterprise.

Environmental Aspects

The ISO 14001 standard says:

4.3.1 Environmental aspects

The organization shall establish, implement and maintain a procedure(s)

a) to identify the environmental aspects of its activities, products and services within the defined scope of the environmental management system that it can control and those that it can influence taking into account planned or new developments, or new or modified activities, products and services, and

---

b) to determine those aspects that have or can have significant impact(s) on the environment (i.e. significant environmental aspects).

The organization shall document this information and keep it up to date.

The organization shall ensure that the significant environmental aspects are taken into account in establishing, implementing and maintaining its environmental management system.

During this initial review, you should also make sure you have identified any legal requirements (environmental regulations, permits, corporate or company policies) that relate to these environmental aspects. I'll cover that process a little later in this section.

As a reminder, here is an official ISO definition of *environmental aspect*:

> **The elements of an organization's activities, products and services that can interact with the environment are called environmental aspects. Examples include a discharge, an emission, consumption or reuse of a material, or generation of noise.**

And here is the official ISO definition of *environmental impact*:

> **Changes to the environment, either adverse or beneficial, that result wholly or partially from environmental aspects are called environmental impacts. Examples of adverse impacts include pollution of air, and depletion of natural resources. Examples of beneficial impacts include improved water or soil quality. The relationship between environmental aspects and associated impacts is one of cause and effect.**

The standard asks you to collect this information, evaluate the significance of the impacts, document the information, review it periodically, and keep it up to date.

In Chapter 3 on Sustainability Practices you conducted an analysis to figure out which of your impacts could be considered significant. This is an important step, because under ISO 14001 your entire environmental management system is geared toward dealing with those significant impacts. The idea is that while it may be *nice* to deal with the lesser ones, it is *crucial* to your enterprise to deal with those that are significant.

Here you will do things a little more formally, and document the results for ongoing use as you design and implement your environmental management system.

The ISO 14004 EMS Guidance contains the following suggestions for conducting this step:

> To identify and have an understanding of its environmental aspects, an organization should collect quantitative
> and/or qualitative data on the characteristics of its activities, products and services such as inputs and outputs
> of materials or energy, processes and technology used, facilities and locations, transportation methods and human factors (e.g. impaired vision or hearing). In addition it can be useful to collect information on
>
> a) cause and effect relationships between elements of its activities, products, and services and possible or actual changes to the environment,

b) environmental concerns of interested parties, and

c) possible environmental aspects identified in government regulations and permits, in other standards, or by industry associations, academic institutions, etc.

That's what you did with the sticky notes, remember?

And here is what the guidance says about the process of getting the information and sorting it out:

The process of identifying environmental aspects will benefit from the participation of those individuals who are familiar with the organization's activities, products and services. Although there is no single approach for identifying environmental aspects, the approach selected can for example consider
—emissions to air,
—releases to water,
—releases to land,
—use of raw materials and natural resources (e.g. land use, water use),
—local/community environmental issues,
—use of energy,
—energy emitted (e.g. heat, radiation, vibration),
—waste and by-products, and
—physical attributes (e.g. size, shape, colour, appearance).

Consideration should therefore be given to aspects related to the organization's activities, products and services, such as
—design and development,
—manufacturing processes,
—packaging and transportation,
—environmental performance and practices of contractors, and suppliers,
—waste management,
—extraction and distribution of raw materials and natural resources,
—distribution, use and end of life, and
—wildlife and biodiversity.

And about evaluation for significance:

An understanding of an organization's environmental impacts is necessary when identifying environmental aspects and determining their significance. Many approaches are available. An organization should choose one that suits its needs.
The approach chosen should be capable of recognizing
a) positive (beneficial) as well as negative (adverse) environmental impacts,
b) actual and potential environmental impacts,
c) the part(s) of the environment that might be affected, such as air, water, soil, flora, fauna, cultural heritage, etc.,
d) the characteristics of the location that might affect the impact such as local weather conditions, height of water table, soil types, etc., and
e) the nature of the changes to the environment (such as global vs. local issues, length of time for which the impact occurs, potential for impact to accumulate in strength over time).

When establishing criteria for significance, an organization should consider the following:
a) environmental criteria (such as scale, severity and duration of the impact, or type, size and frequency of an environmental aspect);

b) applicable legal requirements (such as emission and discharge limits in permits or regulations, etc.);
c) the concerns of internal and external interested parties (such as those related to organizational values, public image, noise, odour or visual degradation).

Significance criteria can be applied either to an organization's environmental aspects or to their associated impacts. Environmental criteria can apply to both environmental aspects and environmental impacts, but in most situations they apply to environmental impacts. When applying criteria, an organization can set levels (or values) of significance associated with each criterion, for example based on a combination of likelihood (probability/frequency) of an occurrence and its consequences (severity/intensity). Some type of scale or ranking can be helpful in assigning significance, for example quantitatively in terms of a numeric value, or qualitatively in terms of levels such as high, medium, low or negligible.

An organization may choose to evaluate the significance of an environmental aspect and associated impacts, and may find it useful to combine results from the criteria. It should decide which environmental aspects are significant, e.g. by using a threshold value.

To facilitate planning, an organization should maintain appropriate information on the environmental aspects
identified and those considered significant. The organization should use this information to understand the need for and to determine operational controls. Information on identified impacts should be included as appropriate. It should be reviewed and updated periodically, and when circumstances change to ensure it is up to date. For these purposes, it can be helpful to maintain them in a list, register, database or other form.

I told you there would be plenty of excerpts from the standard!

Really, I can't think of a simpler way to tell you what it says than just to have you read it for yourself.

As you go through this activity, ask yourself (and your groups of helpers) these questions:

- How would you choose which items to select for detailed review?

- What specific methods would you use to identify and evaluate the severity of environmental impacts?

- Who in your organization has had this responsibility up until now?

- What are the criteria you use for comparing the significance of environmental impacts?

If the answer is "I don't know" or "none," you have just identified something for your "to do" list. You can think that one purpose of an environmental management system is to get through that "to do" list: get these questions answered, write the answers down, and tell everyone what they are.

Legal and Other Requirements

The ISO 14001 standard states:

4.3.2 Legal and other requirements

The organization shall establish, implement and maintain a procedure(s)

a) to identify and have access to the applicable legal requirements and other requirements to which the organization subscribes related to its environmental aspects, and

b) to determine how these requirements apply to its environmental aspects.

The organization shall ensure that these applicable legal requirements and other requirements to which the organization subscribes are taken into account in establishing, implementing and maintaining its environmental
management system.

This part of the standard requires that you identify and have *access* to all legal requirements that relate to environmental aspects of your activities, products, or services. It does not require that you actually have copies of such requirements on hand, but most organizations will want to acquire and keep copies of items that are directly relevant to its operations.

Examples of such requirements include:

- those specific to the activity (e.g., site operating permits)

- those specific to the organization's products or services (e.g., company policies)

- those specific to the organization's industry (e.g., codes of ethics or conduct)

- general environmental laws and regulations (e.g., Clean Air Act, Clean Water Act)

- specific authorizations, licenses, and permits (elevator permits, RCRA waste permit)

Do this:

• In your staff group, brainstorm a list of relevant legal and other requirements for your organization's activities, products, or services. Which ones would you want to make sure you have copies of close at hand?

• How would you ensure their accessibility?

• How would you keep track of changes in legal and other requirements?

• Who is (or should be) responsible for this task in your organization?

Think about the following items when collecting this information:

✓ Process (activities, products, or services) name
✓ Process description
✓ Location of process
✓ Frequency of process
✓ Personnel involved
✓ Nature of administrative controls
✓ Environmental aspect
✓ Environmental impact
✓ Legal or other regulatory requirements

These data can be displayed on a spreadsheet format, as in the example below:

Process Name	Descr.	Location	Freq.	Personnel	Admin. Controls	Env Aspect	Env. Impact	Legal & Reg.
1.0	Describe overall process	Where does it occur?	How often?	Who does it?	What admin. controls exist?	How does it relate to the environment	What is the impact on those aspects?	What laws and regs apply?
1.1	Describe sub-process	Where	When	Who	How	Environment aspects	Impacts	Laws and regs
2.0	Describe the process	Where	When	Who	How	Environment aspects	Impacts	Laws and regs

Question 2: Where Do We Want to Go?

Here is where you get to play with developing an environmental policy. This is the "first step" as described in the standards because developing a policy statement, with its related objectives and targets, is the essential foundation for a comprehensive environmental management system.

Based on the data gathered and analyzed in answer to the "where are we now?" question, earlier, this step creates the framework for the organization's overall environmental management system. The policy is based on your earlier work identifying aspects, impacts, and legal and other requirements.

The ISO 14001 standard states:

4.2 Environmental policy
Top management shall define the organization's environmental policy and ensure that, within the defined scope
of its environmental management system, it

a) is appropriate to the nature, scale and environmental impacts of its activities, products and services,
b) includes a commitment to continual improvement and prevention of pollution,
c) includes a commitment to comply with applicable legal requirements and with other requirements to which
the organization subscribes which relate to its environmental aspects,
d) provides the framework for setting and reviewing environmental objectives and targets,
e) is documented, implemented and maintained,
f) is communicated to all persons working for or on behalf of the organization, and
g) is available to the public.

That's it.

YOU get to decide what goes in your policy (but notice the standard does require you to commit to compliance, continual improvement, and pollution prevention): how to set and review environmental objectives and targets (and which targets to set), how to document it, how to carry it out, how to maintain it, how to communicate it to your employees, and how to make it available to the public.

The only requirement is that you actually DO whatever it is you say you will do. Not just talk about it, or hire a consultant and spend a lot of time in meetings, or distribute little laminated wallet cards to all your employees with the "policy" on them (which most of them never heard about until the wallet card appeared in their pay envelope).

The ISO 14004 guidance makes some practical suggestions, too:

In developing its environmental policy, an organization should consider

a) its mission, vision, core values and beliefs;
b) coordination with other organizational policies (e.g. quality, occupational health and safety);
c) the requirements of, and communication with, interested parties;
d) guiding principles;
e) specific local or regional conditions;
f) its commitments to prevention of pollution and continual improvement;
g) its commitment to comply with legal requirements and other requirements to which the organization subscribes.

Developing the Policy

Because the environmental policy must be "defined by top management," it is often tempting to simply have top management write the policy. Executive and lower level staff often have valuable insights, however, especially about the nature, scale, and environmental impacts of the facility operations, and should be explicitly included in the process. If the facility is large enough to have a dedicated environmental staff, the head of that department can draft the policy for top management review and approval.

Importance of Aspects and Impacts

Remember, the policy is supposed to help deal with the significant environmental impacts identified as part of the initial review and legal review. Therefore it is vital to make sure that all significant environmental impacts are identified, and that all significant environmental impacts are included in the policy.

This does not require a lengthy "laundry list" of items, but it does require that you invest the time and effort to do a thorough and useful initial review, so that the policy can actually help accomplish your most important environmental goals.

For example, if water usage is a significant environmental impact, put it in the environmental policy if you want to make sure it is controlled effectively. If there are important compliance issues associated with water quality, put those in the policy as well. Remember that the policy should function to help you meet the goals you set. It can always be changed over time, as the result of management review and changing circumstances, but it should be designed as a useful document and not just something used once to meet an outside requirement.

Continual vs. Continuous Improvement

Notice that the ISO 14001 standard requires *continual* improvement, not *continuous* improvement. In English, these words signify very different things, as illustrated in Figure 4.3, below.

Continuous improvement (Line B) signifies moment-to-moment, day-by-day improvement of performance in the same area, against some measurement standard. For example, if water quality measurements today show a certain number of ppm (parts per million) of tds (total dissolved solids), tomorrow they should show a measurable improvement. This is very difficult to accomplish, especially as each successive increment of improvement becomes more technically difficult and therefore more costly to achieve.

Continual improvement (Line A) signifies an upward-trending movement, such that the overall direction is toward the desired goal. As shown in Figure 4.3, this is more easily and realistically accomplished through the use of specific projects (contained on an action plan) to meet specific objectives and targets.

The definition of continual improvement in the ISO 14001 standard is as follows:

[The] process of enhancing the environmental management system to achieve improvements in overall environmental performance in line with the organization's environmental policy. Note: The process need not take place in all areas of activity simultaneously.

For example, under the concept of continual improvement, you can bring a new sewage treatment plant on line to deal with issues of water quality, and later install a new incinerator to deal with issues of air emissions. You could also begin to computerize your measurements, install energy-saving key tags for guest rooms, contract with a local piggery to receive food wastes, and purchase cloth laundry bags for guest rooms to replace plastic ones uses previously. All of these projects contribute to the continual improvement of your system, to enhance environmental performance. Yet all are in different environmental areas, meet different objectives and targets, and many are in different functional areas of your facility, as well.

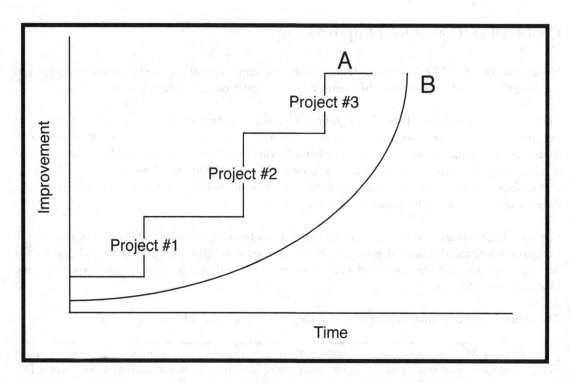

Figure 4.3. Line A represents *continual* improvement, where Projects #1, 2 and 3 each contribute to the improvement of environmental performance and the meeting of objectives and targets. Line B represents *continuous* improvement, a moment-by-moment incremental performance improvement.

Therefore, it is important to make sure that the ISO 14001 requirements are explicitly addressed in the policy. The easiest way to do that is to simply repeat the required language in your policy, along with any facility-specific or corporate-specific language that may already be present.

So, make sure that somewhere in your policy the following statements (or their equivalents in your own words) can be found:

- "The XYZ Hotel is committed to continual improvement of its environmental management system performance and to prevention of pollution."
- "The XYZ Hotel is committed to compliance with relevant environmental legislation and regulations"
- "The XYZ Hotel is committed to compliance with the following other requirements to which it subscribes:" [list these, such as any local or international "green hotel" programs, or Sustainable Slopes or The Natural Step, or any other industry-specific environmental programs in which you participate]
- "This environmental policy is intended to provide a framework for setting and reviewing environmental objectives and targets"
- "This environmental policy is documented, implemented and maintained and communicated to all employees through periodic trainings, posting in staff areas, and [other methods used, such as newsletters, annual contests, etc.]"
- "This environmental policy is available to the public through posting in the reception area and each guest room" [or however you choose to make it available].

You can also include statements about quality of service, guest amenities, focus on ecotourism or social and community relations, profitability, mission/vision statements, etc. These are all worthwhile, helpful, and perhaps even necessary to satisfy other kinds of needs and requirements.

But the statements above are *required* to ensure that your policy is in conformance with the ISO 14001 standard, which after all is the point of this activity!

Here is a checklist of questions you can use as you develop (or review) your policy:

Environmental Policy Checklist

❑ What specific statements in your policy relate to the nature, scale, and significant environmental impacts of your organization's activities, products and services?

❑ Where is the commitment to continual improvement found in the policy?

❑ Where is the commitment to prevention of pollution found in the policy?

❑ Where is the commitment to compliance with relevant environmental legislation and regulations found in the policy?

❑ Where is the commitment to compliance with other relevant requirements to which your organization subscribes found in the policy? Where is the list of those other requirements found in the policy?

❑ Where is the description of how your environmental policy is documented?

❑ Where is the description of how your environmental policy is maintained?

❑ Where is the description of how your environmental policy is implemented? [You should point to an environmental manual or procedure guide for # 6, 7, and 8]

❑ Where is the description of how your environmental policy is communicated to all employees? [Remember that you may need to translate it into one or more languages to ensure all employees can access and understand it]

❑ Where is the description of how your environmental policy is made available to the public? [i.e., guests and stakeholders]

On the following pages you will find a sample environmental policy, based on the ISO standard, and a tool I call the Hospitality Forever™ Policy Builder, which comprises a template you can use to build your environmental policy. Here is how to use the Hospitality Forever™ Policy Builder:

Instructions for the Hospitality Forever™ Policy Builder

Panel 1: Results of Initial Review
1. List the significant environmental aspects of your business unit
2. List the significant environmental impacts these aspects have
3. List any legal or other requirements your business unit must meet
4. List any industry standards your business unit has adopted

Panel 2: Draft Environmental Policy
1. List the significant environmental aspects you have chosen to address during this planning cycle
2. List the significant environmental impacts you have chosen to address during this planning cycle
3. List the legal or other requirements you must meet
4. List the industry standards you have adopted

Panel 3: Review Draft Environmental Policy

Solicit comments on the Draft Environmental Policy from:
- Staff
- Local community
- Customers
- Management
- Investors or stockholders
- Regulatory agencies
- Landowners
- Permit-grantors
- others???

Panel 4: Final Environmental Policy
Make sure you have at least the minimum 7 statements that address the standard (see sample policy below). You may also want to include statements of your organization's mission, values, overall environmental goals, monitoring and measurement program, and community relations principles. Some organizations include statements about industry leadership or contribution to the community.

[Sample] Environmental Policy
The [xx] Hotel

1. The [xx] Hotel is committed to providing high quality hospitality and service to our guests and protecting, maintaining and enhancing the environment which our guests come to enjoy, and in which our staff live and work. [If a unit of a larger organization, refer to corporate policy, or mission/vision statement here also.]

2. To accomplish this policy, the [xx] Hotel is committed to continual improvement and prevention of pollution. We seek to reduce the significant environmental impacts of our operations through [put specific actions here; for example, minimizing usage of nonrenewable energy, minimizing water usage, and minimizing usage of toxic, hazardous, and non-biodegradable chemicals and other materials, and by maximizing reuse and recycling wherever possible].

3. The [xx] Hotel is committed to complying with relevant environmental legislation and other environmental requirements. We subscribe to the principles of [list here appropriate industry associations, "green" organizations to which it belongs, chamber of commerce environmental policies, etc.]

4. The [xx] Hotel periodically [specify interval; e.g., annually] reviews its environmental objectives and targets to ensure they assist in meeting the intent of this policy and are appropriate to the nature, scale, and environmental impacts of our activities, products and services.

5. This policy is documented and implemented through our environmental manual, procedures and specific work instructions; maintained through [annual] top management reviews and any necessary revisions.

6. This policy is communicated to all employees in their native language through periodic formal and informal training [specify method: classroom, on-the-job, apprenticeships, daily briefings, bulletin board, newsletter, etc.]. This policy is posted in work areas [specify language, e.g., in English and other local language(s), if applicable].

7. This policy is available to the public and to our guests; it is posted in our Reception area and in all guest rooms [specify appropriate language(s)].

Signed:
Title:
Date/Version:

Note: These paragraphs correspond to the following requirements of ISO 14001:

Policy Paragraph Number	ISO 14001 Requirement
1	4.2.a: appropriate to the nature, scale and environmental impacts
2	4.2.b: a commitment to continual improvement and prevention of pollution
3	4.2.c: a commitment to comply with applicable legal and other requirements
4	4.2.d: framework for setting and reviewing environmental objectives/targets
5	4.2.e: documented, implemented, maintained
6	4.2.f: communicated to all persons working for/on behalf of organization
7	4.2.g: available to the public

Here is a first draft of an environmental policy from one of my clients, which was one of the first hotels in south Asia to seek ISO 14001 certification (English is not the first language of any of the staff):

[This resort] is an eco-friendly tourist resort committed to protect the environment.

We protect the natural habitat where the business operates and conduct our business in an environmentally friendly manner, by efficiently using our resources – water and energy – and effectively managing our waste – solid and liquid waste and emissions – to minimize the impact on the environs and human beings.
By regular meetings and written communications, we make our employees, guests, suppliers and the public aware of our objectives. We evolve and maintain systems, which will be continually improved and reviewed periodically to achieve the short term and long term objectives.

We undertake to comply with the expectations of the Public and Government legislation in meeting the environmental concerns.

Let's Save Mother Earth!

Pretty good for a first effort, and I guarantee that everyone from the launderers and the groundskeepers on up participated in drafting it. By the way, it is now published in two of the three national languages, and posted (in both languages) in all of the work areas.

Do you think they are proud of their accomplishment? Do you think everyone who participated will be willing – even excited – to do what they can to help it succeed? Do you understand why, although top management has to be responsible for the policy, they cannot be the sole authors of it?

OK. On to the next set of tasks.

Environmental
Aspects:

Environmental
Impacts:

Legal
requirements:

Industry
standards:

Results of Initial Review

The HF Policy Builder™

Part I

Aspects to
Address:

Impacts to
Address:

Legal requirements to
meet:

Industry standards to
adopt:

Draft Environmental Policy

The HF Policy Builder™

Part II

Aspects to
Address:

Impacts to
Address:

Legal requirements to
meet:

Industry standards to
adopt:

Draft Environmental Policy

Consider Input from:
• staff
• community
• management (board)
• regulatory
• other?

Mission

Statement of Environmental Goals:

Aspects to Address:

Impacts to Address:

Legal requirements to meet:

Industry standards to adopt:

Communication with
Stakeholders:

Community Relations:

Monitoring and Measurement:

Commitment to Management
Review:

Commitment to Continual
Improvement:

Final Environmental Policy

Developing Objectives, Targets and Programs

These are the specifics that will become part of your environmental management program: they constitute the actual description of "where are we going?" that will lead to developing action items that specific staff members will carry out during the journey.

The ISO 14001 standard characterizes them this way:

4.3.3 Objectives, targets and programme(s)

The organization shall establish, implement and maintain documented environmental objectives and targets, at
relevant functions and levels within the organization.

The objectives and targets shall be measurable, where practicable, and consistent with the environmental policy, including the commitments to prevention of pollution, to compliance with applicable legal requirements
and with other requirements to which the organization subscribes, and to continual improvement.

When establishing and reviewing its objectives and targets, an organization shall take into account the legal requirements and other requirements to which the organization subscribes, and its significant environmental aspects. It shall also consider its technological options, its financial, operational and business requirements, and the views of interested parties.

The organization shall establish, implement and maintain a programme(s) for achieving its objectives and targets. Programme(s) shall include

a) designation of responsibility for achieving objectives and targets at relevant functions and levels of the organization, and
b) the means and time-frame by which they are to be achieved.

The "standard" EMS diagram (and the ISO standard) classifies this set of tasks as "Planning," and that is exactly right. You are beginning to move from "what do we want?" to "how to we accomplish it?," which is a planning type of function.

But I have included this set of tasks here with the "Where do we want to go?" Big Question because you are still just developing your goals, not operationalizing them. You are still figuring out what you want, only now you are assigning specific numbers (how many kilowatt hours will you save per month?), performance expectations (specific targets), and staff (the housekeeping department, the Director of Guest Services, the Lead Groundskeeper) to the job.

There are many parts to the "How do we get there?" question, which I will get to soon enough. Remember my Principle #1, "Keep it Sweet and Simple"? That's what I am trying to do here. If you take this process one step at a time, in a logical order, you'll find it is not so scary after all.

To begin developing your objectives, consider all those things you have pulled together for your analysis of aspects and impacts, and creation of your policy:

> ✓ legal and other requirements
> ✓ significant environmental aspects
> ✓ technological options
> ✓ financial, operational and business requirements

✓ views of interested parties

Remember your objectives and targets need to be consistent with the environmental policy, including commitment to pollution prevention and continual improvement.

Objectives and targets also usually need *performance indicators* so you can measure your progress toward achieving them. Review the following examples:

Objective	Target	Performance Indicator
• Reduce kitchen waste going to landfill	• 10% reduction annually	• Quantity of waste per day -- as measured in pounds, gallons, etc.
• Reduce energy use	• 5% reduction annually	• Amount of energy used per week, as measured in kwh, tons, $$$, etc.
• Reduce environmental penalties and fines	• Zero criminal prosecutions	• Number of prosecutions
• Improve wildlife habitat	• 10% increase in selected wildlife species	• Number of species or individuals, acres of land set aside, etc.

Also consider the suggestions in the ISO 14004 Guidance:

4.3.3.1 Setting objectives and targets

In setting objectives and targets, an organization should consider several inputs, including

a) principles and commitments in its environmental policy,
b) its significant environmental aspects (and information developed in determining them),
c) applicable legal requirements and other requirements to which the organization subscribes,
d) effects of achieving objectives on other activities and processes,
e) views of interested parties,
f) technological options and feasibility,
g) financial, operational, and organizational considerations, including information from suppliers and contractors,
h) possible effects on the public image of the organization,
i) findings from environmental reviews, and
j) other organizational goals.
[....]
An objective can be expressed directly as a specific performance level, or may be expressed in a general manner and further defined by one or more targets. When targets are set, they should be measurable by performance levels that need to be met to ensure the achievement of the related objectives. Targets may need
to include a specified time frame to be delivered by the programme.

An acronym many planners find useful when developing targets is to remember to make them SMART:

Specific**M**easurable **A**chievable **R**ealistic **T**imely = SMART

So your "objective-setting" analysis could have the following components:

Objective	Specific	Measurable	Achievable	Realistic	Timely
Save energy	Electricity use in guest rooms	Decrease 5%	Yes, if we install key tags and brief the guests and staff	We need to train our guests and staff – we'll see!	Seek an annual decrease; measure monthly usage by building wing
Save water	Landscape water on lawn	Decrease 5%	Yes, through timing and use of drip system; explore upgrading to drought-resistant grass species or replacing with native ground cover	Need to train the staff to make this work.	Measure by month, compare costs of seasonal usage and upgrading
Etc.					

Question 3: How Do We Get There?

Here is where the rubber meets the road, as they say. Now you will begin to define the staff roles and responsibilities, train them to take action, communicate with the outside world, develop procedures and document them, figure out how to handle emergencies, and in general get organized to carry out your policy. This means putting together a real environmental management program to reach your objectives and targets.

Don't worry yet about how well the program works; that part comes later, in the "Are We Getting There?" section; right now, invest your time designing something you think will work OK:

remember "continual improvement"? This is what it means: try something, measure your results, correct your course if you need to.

The 1996 ISO 14001 standard contained instructions and guidance for developing the *program* aspect of your system that have been dropped from the 2004 standard (probably because they seemed redundant for the tens of thousands of enterprises worldwide that had developed systems by 2004). I think this information continues to be very helpful for those just starting out, however, and so it is included here.

Develop an Environmental Management Program

The 1996 ISO 14001 standard, Section 4.3.4, required an organization to establish and maintain a comprehensive program to accomplish its objectives and targets. This program includes:

❑ designation of responsibility for achieving objectives and targets at each relevant function and level of the organization, and

❑ the means and time frame by which the objectives and targets will be achieved.

The program relates to both existing and new or modified activities, products, or services, and should be revised as needed to ensure that it continues to apply to such activities, products, or services.

A comprehensive environmental management program should be integrated into an organization's strategic management planning process, and should prioritize as well as identify specific actions that will help improve an organization's environmental performance. In fact, actions may relate to individual processes, projects, products, services, sites, or facilities within a site; the key lies in strategic, dynamic, comprehensive program design.

Guidance contained in the 1996 version of ISO 14004, Section 4.2.6, included the following questions to ask while developing your environmental management program:

Some Issues to be Considered in Environmental Management Programs

1. What is the organization's process for developing environmental management programs?

2. Does the environmental management planning process involve all responsible parties?

3. Is there a process for periodic reviews of the program?

4. How do these programs address the issues of resources, responsibility, timing, and priority?

5. How are the environmental management programs responsive to the environmental policy and general planning activities?

6. How are the environmental management programs monitored and revised?

Here is a kind of table you could construct, to organize your thoughts (this example is based on one from the 1996 ISO 14004 guidance):

Policy	Objective	Target	Program Component	Action
• Conserve natural resources	• Minimize water use whenever technically and commercially practical	• Reduce water consumption in landscape by 15% of present levels within one year.	Water reuse	• Install equipment to recycle rinse water from kitchen for re-use in garden • Water only at twilight, not in the heat of the day • As equipment is replaced, replace with drippers rather than sprayers
Etc.				

Now let's return to the present, and to the 2004 ISO requirements for your system. There are seven:

1. Resources, Roles, Responsibility and Authority
2. Competence, Training and Awareness
3. Communication
4. Documentation
5. Control of Documents
6. Operational Control
7. Emergency Preparedness and Response

I'll take them one by one.

Resources, Roles, Responsibility and Authority

Who is going to carry out this wonderful new policy? Put another way, whose head will roll if actions don't get taken, if targets are not met, if objectives get forgotten, if the policy merely sits on a shelf rather than getting applied day to day?

Whose fault is it if the guest uses the hang tag, but the linens are washed anyway?

The fault lies – always – with top management.

As former US President Harry S. Truman famously said, "The buck stops here!" While it may have been someone on the housekeeping staff who actually ignored the tag, collected the linens, and deposited them in the laundry, it is top management's job to develop and manage the *system*. If the system is broken, it is top management's job to get it fixed.

It is also top management's job to make sure the staff have the money, equipment, support, staff, and time to actually do what the policy promised would be done.

Here's how the 2004 ISO 14001 standard puts it:

4.4.1 Resources, roles, responsibility and authority

Management shall ensure the availability of resources essential to establish, implement, maintain and improve the environmental management system. Resources include human resources and specialized skills, organizational infrastructure, technology and financial resources.

Roles, responsibilities and authorities shall be defined, documented and communicated in order to facilitate effective environmental management.

The organization's top management shall appoint a specific management representative(s) who, irrespective of other responsibilities, shall have defined roles, responsibilities and authority for

a) ensuring that an environmental management system is established, implemented and maintained in accordance with the requirements of this International Standard,
b) reporting to top management on the performance of the environmental management system for review, including recommendations for improvement.

What do I mean by "resources"? I'll let the ISO 14004 guidance shed some light on that topic:

When identifying the resources needed to establish, implement and maintain the environmental management system, an organization should consider
—infrastructure,
—information systems,
—training,
—technology, and
—financial, human and other resources specific to its operations.

You may have realized by now that you often will have to cycle back through previous steps in light of subsequent steps, at least the first time you develop an environmental management system.

Remember the columns labeled "achievable" and "realistic" in your SMART analysis of objectives and targets?

Well, if you don't allocate the necessary resources, the targets are not achievable. If you can't *get* the necessary resources (money, staff, equipment, time) they are not realistic. So get out the old pencil and paper, and go back and spend some time developing objectives and targets that *are* achievable and realistic.

What if you are a small resort, or bistro, or tour operator, or bed-and-breakfast inn, and don't have a big budget or staff or lots of technical knowledge about environmental stuff? As always, the ISO 14004 guidance has some suggestions:

Practical help — Human, physical and financial resources

The resource base and organizational structure of a small or medium-sized enterprise (SME) can impose certain limitations on environmental management system implementation. To overcome these limitations, an SME can consider cooperative strategies with

a) larger client and supplier organizations, to share technology and knowledge,

b) other SMEs in a supply chain or local basis to define and address common issues, share experiences, facilitate technical development, use facilities jointly, and collectively engage external resources,
c) standardization organizations, SME associations, chambers of commerce, for training and awareness programmes, and
d) universities and other research centres, to support productivity improvements and innovation.

What this means is that if you don't have all the resources you would like, partner with (or even create) an entity that does. For example, many small communities have very active tourist bureaus that can put together training programs, or share seasonal equipment, or centralize recycling facilities, or even conduct fundraising campaigns. Again, by involving the community in your environmental management system, you can often solve problems before they begin.

Unless your operation is very small indeed, you will have staff: employees, contractors, suppliers. Who should do what in this new world of environmental management systems?

For example, what should be the roles and responsibilities of the General Manager, the Hotel Manager, the Maintenance Manager, the Head Groundskeeper, the Housekeeping Staff, the Front Desk Manager, the Tour Operator, the Kitchen Steward, the Sous-Chef, the Chair Lift Operator, the Resort Naturalist, the Marketing Director, the Bussing Staff, the Dishwasher? To put it another way, if you have sat through the credits of any recent movie, you have seen credit given to the person I call the "Foley Artist's Gaffer's Accountant's Hairdresser's Caterer's Driver's Special Effects Team" – in other words, *everybody* who is connected with the enterprise has a role, a responsibility, and gets some credit.

It should be the same way in your enterprise.

The chart below is a way of thinking about how to structure the responsibilities and authority for an organization (from the ISO 14004 guidance):

Example of environmental responsibilities	Typical person(s) responsible
Establish overall direction	President, chief executive officer (CEO), Board of directors
Develop environmental policy	President, CEO, and others as appropriate
Develop environmental objectives, targets and Programmes	Relevant managers
Monitor overall environmental management system performance	Chief environmental manager
Assure compliance with applicable legal requirements and other requirements to which the organization subscribes	All managers
Promote continual improvement	All managers
Identify customers' expectations	Sales and marketing staff
Identify requirements for suppliers	Purchasers, buyers

Develop and maintain accounting procedures	Finance/accounting managers
Conform to environmental management system requirements	All persons working for or on behalf of the organization
Review the operation of the environmental management system	Top management
NOTE Companies and institutions have different organizational structures and need to define environmental management responsibilities based on their own work processes. In the case of an SME, for example, the owner can be the person responsible for all of these activities.	

Competence, Training and Awareness

This bit is the key, of course, to making it all happen. The people who actually do the work must be as competent as you can make them: through education and experience qualifications; initial and ongoing training; and activities designed to make them aware of the environmental policy and practices, and their responsibilities in carrying them out.

The hang tag problem is a symptom of a special failure in this arena: the staff clearly are not trained in what to do, and my guess is they are probably not aware of how their actions relate to your environmental policy or how they affect the accomplishment of your objectives and targets. Do they even know about the policy, or about the objectives and targets?

Again, here is the language from the ISO14001 standard:

4.4.2 Competence, training and awareness

The organization shall ensure that any person(s) performing tasks for it or on its behalf that have the potential to cause a significant environmental impact(s) identified by the organization is (are) competent on the basis of
appropriate education, training or experience, and shall retain associated records.

The organization shall identify training needs associated with its environmental aspects and its environmental management system. It shall provide training or take other action to meet these needs, and shall retain associated records.

The organization shall establish, implement and maintain a procedure(s) to make persons working for it or on its behalf aware of

a) the importance of conformity with the environmental policy and procedures and with the requirements of the environmental management system,
b) the significant environmental aspects and related actual or potential impacts associated with their work, and the environmental benefits of improved personal performance,
c) their roles and responsibilities in achieving conformity with the requirements of the environmental management system, and
d) the potential consequences of departure from specified procedures.

How you accomplish these tasks is up to you.

✔ Do you require new hires to go through an employee orientation program that contains information on your environmental management system?

✔ Do you publish a self-paced training manual on your environmental program?

✔ Do you conduct brown-bag lunch meetings to discuss your environmental management system and how each department fits in?

✔ Do you put copies of the policy in staff pay envelopes?

✔ Do you contract with outside trainers to run periodic live training workshops on site for each department?

✔ Do you post the relevant objectives and targets in each work area?

✔ Do you have an apprentice program for new hires?

✔ Do you hand out laminated wallet cards to all employees?

✔ Do you brief new suppliers or contractors on how you expect them to participate?

✔ Do you have different training programs for different levels of staff?

✔ Do you have training for both Part-time and Full-time staff?

✔ Do you have a way to handle staff turnover (the person you trained yesterday may not be the person doing the work today)?

✔ Do you have a way to document the training you have accomplished: who, what, when?

If *you* are top, middle, and front line "management" as well as the entire staff, how competent are you to take this whole project on? Do *you* need some training, mentoring, books to read?

The Training Needs Matrix below points out the various kinds of training you may need to develop, and the various audiences that should attend.

Training Needs Matrix

Type of Training	Purpose	Audience
Raising awareness of the strategic importance of environmental management	To gain commitment and alignment to the organization's environmental policy	Senior Management
Raising general environmental awareness	To gain commitment to the environmental policy, objectives and targets and to instill a sense of individual responsibility	All employees
Skills enhancement	Improve performance in specific areas -- operations, R&D, engineering, etc.	Employees with environmental responsibilities
Compliance	Ensure regulatory and internal requirements for training are met	Employees whose actions can affect compliance
Specific task training	To teach specific skills necessary to perform tasks correctly	All employees whose tasks relate to environmental objectives and targets (hint: this means everyone)

Contractors and other non-employee personnel may need training also. As the ISO 14004 guidance points out, it is important to have **evidence** that contractors have the requisite knowledge and skills to perform their work in an "environmentally responsible manner" as called for in standard contract clauses.

Communication

The main thrust of this part is *internal* communication: how do you communicate among yourselves? Does the purchasing department know to alert other departments when one department has ordered new light bulbs, so they can consolidate the order? Does the kitchen staff know to talk to the housekeeping staff when trying out new cleaners? Does anyone ever talk to maintenance except when there is an emergency?

You need to have – you guessed it, a *process* – to make this work well. And the process has to be documented, so someone else can find it and follow it. And you need to keep it up to date (do you still fax information to your various departments?).

You also need to have a systematic way of dealing with your customers, suppliers, neighbors, regulators, stockholders, stakeholders, and people who wander in off the street in search of a quality hospitality experience.

The ISO 14001 standard puts it this way:

4.4.3 Communication

With regard to its environmental aspects and environmental management system, the organization shall establish, implement and maintain a procedure(s) for

a) internal communication among the various levels and functions of the organization,
b) receiving, documenting and responding to relevant communication from external interested parties.

The organization shall decide whether to communicate externally about its significant environmental aspects, and shall document its decision. If the decision is to communicate, the organization shall establish and implement a method(s) for this external communication.

And the ISO 14004 guidance provides some examples:

Practical help — Internal and external communication

Examples of information to be communicated include

a) general information about the organization,
b) management statement if applicable,
c) environmental policy, objectives and targets,
d) environmental management processes (including employee and interested party involvement),
e) the organization's commitments to continual improvement and prevention of pollution,
f) information related to environmental aspects of products and services, conveyed through for example environmental labels and declarations,
g) information on the organization's environmental performance including trends (e.g. waste reduction, product stewardship, past performance),
h) the organization's compliance with legal and other requirements to which the organization subscribes, and corrective actions taken in response to identified instances of noncompliance,

---

i) supplementary information in reports, such as glossaries,
j) financial information such as cost savings or investments in environmental projects,
k) potential strategies to improve an organization's environmental performance,
l) information related to environmental incidents, and
m) sources for further information, such as contact person(s) or websites.

For both internal and external environmental communication, it is important to remember that

—information should be understandable and adequately explained,
—information should be traceable,
—the organization should present an accurate picture of its performance,
—if possible, information should be presented in comparable forms (e.g. similar units of measurement).

Remember, this isn't an exercise in empire-building; it is a tool for helping you reach your sustainability goals. Make sure you are talking with your own people, and those on the outside (including customers, suppliers, guests) with whom you interact. Pretty simple, yes?

Documentation

You knew we'd get to this part, didn't you? The ISO 14001 standard requires that all of your procedures be *documented*, or they don't count for certification.

Here's what it says:

4.4.4 Documentation

The environmental management system documentation shall include

a) the environmental policy, objectives and targets,
b) description of the scope of the environmental management system,
c) description of the main elements of the environmental management system and their interaction, and reference to related documents,
d) documents, including records, required by this International Standard, and
e) documents, including records, determined by the organization to be necessary to ensure the effective planning, operation and control of processes that relate to its significant environmental aspects.

I'm just going to let the ISO 14004 guidance speak for itself on this topic:

To ensure that its environmental management system is understood and operating effectively, an organization should develop and maintain adequate documentation. The purpose of such documentation is to provide necessary information to employees and other interested parties as appropriate. Documentation should be collected and maintained in a way that reflects the culture and needs of an organization, building onto and improving its existing information system. The extent of the documentation can differ from one organization to another but it should describe the environmental management system.

An organization may choose to summarize information in the form of a manual, which constitutes an overview
or summary of the environmental management system and can provide direction to related documentation. The structure of any such environmental management system manual need not follow the clause structure of ISO14001 or any other standard.

For effective management of its key processes (i.e. those related to its identified significant environmental aspects), an organization should establish (a) procedure(s) that describe, in appropriate detail, a specified way of carrying out each process. If an organization decides not to document a procedure, appropriate employees need to be informed, through communication or training, of the requirements to be satisfied.

Records, which provide information on results achieved or evidence of activities performed, are part of an organization's documentation, but are generally controlled through different management processes.

Documents can be managed in any medium (paper, electronic, photos, posters) that is useful, legible, easily understood and accessible to those needing the information contained therein. There can be advantages to maintaining documents electronically, such as ease of updating, controlling access, and ensuring that all users are using the valid versions of documents.

I couldn't have said it better.

Notice who is in charge of this ship: you – the Captain and the crew – are! That is the beauty of a voluntary, consensus-based standard: you can choose how much to do of what it says, and you can change your mind at any time. Of course, if you decide *not* to document a procedure in writing now, and find later on such documentation would be helpful, you will have to do it then. But you can choose, steer your own ship as it were, at each step throughout the process.

This is why the environmental management system process is so powerful, too. Rather than giving you a whole bunch of "do's and don'ts" (like practices, for example), it allows you to determine what actions to take based on criteria that are important to you and your enterprise.

Make sure you read this next discussion; it will make you happy.

Here is where a lot of consultants, especially IT consultants, make their money: selling you software to handle the documentation "requirements" of the standard. Here also is where a lot of beginners on the path to sustainability get discouraged because it seems like more of a paperwork exercise than anything truly substantial, or even helpful. Changing light bulbs, now *that's* something you can get your hands on (literally!).

But notice, it is your choice whether, and how much, to document your procedures. It also is your choice how much of your enterprise to put into the environmental management system at the beginning (or indeed at any other time); this is called the "scope" of the environmental management system. Perhaps you only need to work on the food and beverage function now, or housekeeping, or grounds or maintenance. The "or" is important here; that is why I started you off with Practices, and Aspects and Impacts – the Situation Review.

Your policy should be about, and your system should be designed to take care of, your most significant aspects and impacts, especially at the beginning. Karl-Henrik Robért calls these "the low-hanging fruit." Eventually you will want to collect all the fruit (and of course professional fruit pickers know to start at the top, so they have less far to carry the fruit as the work progresses), but when you are just learning it is easier to begin with the fruit that is easiest to reach.

So even if you only identify *one aspect* that has *one impact* (water usage, for example), and figure out a way in *one department* (kitchen, or housekeeping, or landscape) to change *one thing or action* that will make a difference, you are on the path. And as a little book of Buddhist sayings I got in Sri Lanka says, "As long as you are on the right path, all you have to do is keep walking."

OK, take a deep breath and let's go back to the environmental management system process.

Control of Documents

If you decide to document your procedures, you now have to control those documents. Sometimes hole-punching them and putting them in binders is the best way to do that. Sometimes you will want to keep them electronically, or on some "permanent" storage medium. And while you may develop a policy or a system and keep it for many years, sometimes your policy or system will change, and sometimes your storage technology will change, so you have to have a way to keep both the documents and access to the up to date.

The ISO 14001 standard says as much:

4.4.5 Control of documents

Documents required by the environmental management system and by this International Standard shall be controlled. Records are a special type of document and shall be controlled in accordance with the requirements given in the section on control of records.

The organization shall establish, implement and maintain a procedure(s) to

a) approve documents for adequacy prior to issue,
b) review and update as necessary and re-approve documents,
c) ensure that changes and the current revision status of documents are identified,
d) ensure that relevant versions of applicable documents are available at points of use,
e) ensure that documents remain legible and readily identifiable,
f) ensure that documents of external origin determined by the organization to be necessary for the planning and operation of the environmental management system are identified and their distribution controlled, and
g) prevent the unintended use of obsolete documents and apply suitable identification to them if they are retained for any purpose.

If you are a huge organization, with many facilities and locations, you will probably have an entire staff devoted to this function (although they may or may not have anyone who specializes in their *environmental* documents). But most small hospitality facilities, even small chains or franchise operations, probably use some combination of file folders, binders and computer files, and that's perfectly OK if it meets your needs.

So, you should probably create a document numbering system, and a way to circulate drafts for comments before approving them (and a list of who should approve them), and a place to put the resulting documents, and a way to make sure everyone who needs it has the most current version. In short, you need a procedure for handling your procedures.

This is a good way to begin: draft a procedure that will describe how you will manage all your environmental procedures from now on. You will find sample format below, and an example of a simple Restaurant and Bar procedure intended to save electricity by switching off lights when they are not needed.

Sample Procedure

Department:		Document ID:	
Environmental aspect:		Valid until:	
Prepared by:		Approved by:	
Purpose:			
Scope:			
Definitions:			
Personnel:			
Procedure:			
Departures:			
References:			

Sample Procedure – Restaurant and Bar

Department: *Restaurant and Bar*	**Procedure ID:** *RB/2/Energy/1.0/1 June 2008*
Prepared by:	**Approved by:**

Purpose:
To save energy in R&B operations

Scope:
Lobby and pool bars, restaurant, office and conference facilities

Definitions:
none

Personnel:
All R&B staff (specific duties listed below)

Procedure:
1. *Bar (lobby and pool) – Bar man responsible*
    *   *Switch on lights at sunset[1]*
    *   *Switch off lights when last guest leaves[2]*
    *   *Manage light levels with dimmers and section switches according to the number, location, and activities of guests*

2. *Restaurant –Manager responsible*
    *   *Switch on lights at the beginning of posted mealtimes*
    *   *Switch off lights at the end of posted mealtimes*
    *   *Manage light levels with dimmers and section switches according to the number and location of guests*

3. *Office and Conference Room – Staff assistant responsible*
    *   *Switch on lights when needed[3]*
    *   *Switch off lights when no longer needed*

4. *Toilets – Staff assistant responsible*
    1. *Switch on light at 6 A.M.[4]*
    2. *Switch off lights when last guest leaves the area*

Departures:
If these procedures are not followed, objectives and targets will not be met for energy saving.

References:
See Environmental Policy Section 5.2; objectives and targets for FY 2008

---

[1] For many facilities this is more effective than designating a particular clock time, as the time of sunset will vary with the time of year.

[2] Again, rather than setting a specific time, this may save energy as guests may depart earlier than the posted time, yet if a time is posted one will have to remain open until that time.

[3] Consider installing dimmers and sectional wiring in conference room to increase flexibility and enable lights not being used to be dimmed or switched off.

[4] Consider installing motion-sensitive switches in toilets.

Operational Control

What is operational control? It is what makes your whole sustainability program work (or not): it is "how we do things around here" on a daily basis. And it is written down, at least for those operations that make a difference for the environment.

Here is what the ISO 14001 standard says:

4.4.6 Operational control

The organization shall identify and plan those operations that are associated with the identified significant environmental aspects consistent with its environmental policy, objectives and targets, in order to ensure that they are carried out under specified conditions, by

a) establishing, implementing and maintaining a documented procedure(s) to control situations where their absence could lead to deviation from the environmental policy, objectives and targets, and
b) stipulating the operating criteria in the procedure(s), and
c) establishing, implementing and maintaining procedures related to the identified significant environmental aspects of goods and services used by the organization and communicating applicable procedures and requirements to suppliers, including contractors.

Notice the standard specifically includes suppliers and contractors. What good does it do for you to have a policy about water usage, or even objectives and targets and practices designed to reduce usage, if your landscape contractor installs water-hungry non-native plants, or your maintenance contractor fails to fix newly-discovered water leaks immediately?

Operational control is a tool for getting *everyone* to help you walk the walk, not just your direct employees.

The ISO 14004 guidance defines operational control further:

Operational controls can take various forms, such as procedures, work instructions, physical controls, use of trained personnel or any combination of these. The choice of the specific control methods depends on a number of factors, such as the skills and experience of people carrying out the operation and the complexity and environmental significance of the operation itself.

A common approach to establishing operational controls includes

a) choosing a method of control;
b) selecting acceptable operating criteria;
c) establishing procedures, as needed, that define how identified operations are to be planned, carried out and controlled; and
d) documenting these procedures, as needed, in the form of instructions, signs, forms, videos, photos, etc.

Again, you are in charge of this ship. Just understand that if the hang tag program isn't working, this is an operational control failure: were you lacking procedures? work instructions? training? supervision? incentives for the staff? ongoing reminders? measurements? hang tags in the appropriate languages for guests and staff?

Emergency Preparedness and Response

This part isn't about how you will respond to the next tsunami or volcanic eruption or hurricane: you should already have procedures for that, along with good relationships with your local emergency responders.

This part is about how you will identify and respond to situations at your operation that can have and impact on the environment. And yes, if your resort is swamped by a hurricane and you have unsecured fuel or hazardous wastes, that is kind of a double emergency. If your facility is in hurricane (or tsunami or volcano) country, you will have to take that into account when designing your system.

But in general, as with all the other parts of the ISO standard, this section focuses on those aspects of your operation that you can influence or control, and what happens when those controls don't work right, or something gets spilled or contaminated by accident.

Here's what the ISO 14001 standard says:

4.4.7 Emergency preparedness and response

The organization shall establish, implement and maintain a procedure(s) to identify potential emergency situations and potential accidents that can have an impact(s) on the environment and how it will respond to them.

The organization shall respond to actual emergency situations and accidents and prevent or mitigate associated adverse environmental impacts.

The organization shall periodically review and, where necessary, revise its emergency preparedness and response procedures, in particular, after the occurrence of accidents or emergency situations.

The organization shall also periodically test such procedures where practicable.

Pretty straightforward.

Here are some factors to consider when developing the procedure (from ISO 14004):

Practical help — Emergency preparedness and response

It is the responsibility of each organization to establish (an) emergency preparedness and response procedure(s) that suits its own particular needs. In establishing its procedure(s), the organization should include consideration of

a) the nature of on-site hazards (e.g. flammable liquid, storage tanks, compressed gases and measures to be taken in the event of spillages or accidental releases),
b) the most likely type and scale of an emergency situation or accident,
c) the potential for (an) emergency situation(s) or accident(s) at a nearby facility (e.g. plant, road, railway line),
d) the most appropriate method(s) for responding to an accident or emergency situation,
e) the actions required to minimize environmental damage,
f) training of emergency response personnel,
g) emergency organization and responsibilities,
h) evacuation routes and assembly points,
i) a list of key personnel and aid agencies, including contact details (e.g. fire department, spillage clean-up

---

services),
j) the possibility of mutual assistance from neighbouring organizations,
k) internal and external communication plans,
l) mitigation and response action(s) to be taken for different types of accident or emergency situation(s),
m) need for process(es) for a post-accident evaluation to establish and implement corrective and preventive actions,
n) periodic testing of emergency response procedure(s),
o) information on hazardous materials, including each material's potential impact on the environment, and measures to be taken in the event of accidental release,
p) training plans and testing for effectiveness, and
q) process for post-accident evaluation to define corrective and preventive actions.

Chemical factories and hotels are the kinds of enterprises most likely to have good emergency planning, but how many hospitality facilities pay attention to their potential for release of dangerous chemicals?

What if your cleaning solvents got into the local drinking water supply? What if your septic system backed up, or your water treatment plant broke down, or your fertilizer ran off into the swimming pond, or your kitchen caught fire, or the power grid shut down?

A complete environmental management system covers those scenarios, and more. Again, this is an opportunity to involve your staff (and contractors, and perhaps guests) in a vigorous session of "what if?" with the objective of developing specific procedures for who does what and when, in the unlikely event an emergency were to occur.

For example, one of the biggest problems in the aftermath of Hurricane Katrina in the US, and the massive tsunami in south Asia and the earthquake in China, was the quantity of toxic glop that was released into the soil, water, and air. Not only was the event itself devastating in terms of lives and property lost, the cleanup and recovery were made much more difficult because of the ongoing health and safety problems posed by the materials released during and after the event.

So the emergency preparedness part is very important, and must be documented just like any other part of your environmental management system.

Congratulations!

Your environmental management system is mostly set up; certainly the sexy parts are all done now: the policy, objectives and targets, communications – the fun stuff. You are well on your path to sustainability; just keep walking, and you will probably get there.

Now, all you have to do is make sure you are really getting where you want to go, and take corrective action if you are straying too far from the pathway.

Question 4: Are We Getting There?

One way of thinking about these next parts of your system is as the tasks an autopilot would do for you if you were a ship or an airplane: monitor location, measure progress toward the goal (or away from it), correct course when needed, and continuously check all the systems to make sure they are working. Most modern automobiles and computers do these checks when you first turn them on, and they notify you with lights or beeps when something goes wrong as you are using them. I'm going to help you do that for your environmental management system (you'll have to provide your own lights and beeps).

Monitoring and Measurement

What gets measured gets done. Or put another way: if you don't know where you're going, any road will take you there. But you want to make sure you are on the road to sustainability, yes?

You have to figure out what to monitor, and how you will monitor and measure both your environmental management system and your environmental performance. For the purposes of your system, you will focus first on how well you are carrying out the *policy*, and not on how well your actions are protecting and enhancing the *environment*. Once again, the idea is to focus on what you can actually control or influence by your operations: are you following your procedures? are your staff trained and competent? was your environmental management program effective in meeting your target to reduce water usage by 5% during this quarter? Do you need to add or revise any operational controls? Are you paying attention to the significant aspects and impacts of your operation?

So you will be looking both at the *system* and at its *results* as it relates to your objectives and targets. You'll have to figure out other ways to determine whether your targeted 5% reduction in water usage is the "right" number – these measurements simply tell you whether your system got you there or not. This also is not a regulatory compliance audit (that comes later).

Here's how the ISO 14001 standard describes this task:

4.5.1 Monitoring and measurement

The organization shall establish, implement and maintain a procedure(s) to monitor and measure, on a regular basis, the key characteristics of its operations that can have a significant environmental impact. The procedure(s) shall include the documenting of information to monitor performance, applicable operational controls and conformity with the organization's environmental objectives and targets.

The organization shall ensure that calibrated or verified monitoring and measurement equipment is used and maintained and shall retain associated records.

Many hospitality mangers get scared by the terms "monitoring" and "measurement," as if they required some special training or equipment. Nonsense! You already "monitor" if you distribute and collect those guest "smile sheets" ("rate our service from 1 to 5"), and you certainly "measure" if you plan and carry out a budget.

And the ISO 14004 guidance has this to say:

An organization should have a systematic approach for measuring and monitoring its environmental performance on a regular basis. Monitoring involves collecting information, such as measurements or observations, over time. Measurements can be either quantitative or qualitative. Monitoring and measurements can serve many purposes in an environmental management system, such as

a) tracking progress on meeting policy commitments, achieving objectives and targets, and continual improvement,
b) developing information to identify significant environmental aspects,
c) monitoring emissions and discharges to meet applicable legal requirements or other requirements to which the organization subscribes,

---

d) monitoring consumption of water, energy or raw materials to meet objectives and targets,

e) providing data to support or evaluate operational controls,

f) providing data to evaluate the organization's environmental performance, and

g) providing data to evaluate the performance of the environmental management system.

To achieve these purposes, an organization should plan what will be measured, where and when it should be measured, and what methods should be used. To focus resources on the most important measurements, the organization should identify the key characteristics of processes and activities that can be measured and that provide the most useful information.

Yes, you will need a process for this, and you probably should document it in a procedure. But again, you choose what and when and how to do this, and you should focus on the significant aspects of and impacts from your operation. Count what counts!

Evaluation of Compliance

You promised to comply in your policy, didn't you? Well, here's how you prove that it's happening, or find out it's not so you can fix the problem.

The ISO 14001 standard requires:

4.5.2 Evaluation of compliance

4.5.2.1 Consistent with its commitment to compliance, the organization shall establish, implement and maintain a procedure(s) for periodically evaluating compliance with applicable legal requirements.

The organization shall keep records of the results of the periodic evaluations.

4.5.2.2 The organization shall evaluate compliance with other requirements to which it subscribes. The organization may wish to combine this evaluation with the evaluation of legal compliance referred to in 4.5.2.1 or to establish a separate procedure(s).

The organization shall keep records of the results of the periodic evaluations.

Notice some new language: this part of the standard talks about *records*, not *documents*. This distinction is important; I will get to control of records very soon.

Nonconformity, Corrective Action and Preventive Action

What happens if your monitoring and compliance evaluation reveals something bad in your system? Something that is not working right (hang tags, for example)?

"Nonconformity" is a technical term used in the quality assurance field (and some others, such as the environmental management system field) to mean "non-fulfillment of a requirement." If you decide to get your environmental management system actually certified to the ISO standard, the auditor will check to make sure it is in "conformity" with the requirements of the standard: there is a policy, you have documents, you can ensure that your staff is competent, and so forth.

Here you are taking a look at your own operations to find anything that is not in conformity with your environmental management system. After all, you have set a policy, developed objectives and targets, adopted practices based on your aspects and impacts, trained the staff to carry them out – if something is not in conformance with your own requirements, you need to know about it. *Now.*

In fact, that's all the ISO 14001 standard really requires:

4.5.3 Nonconformity, corrective action and preventive action

The organization shall establish, implement and maintain a procedure(s) for dealing with actual and potential nonconformity(ies) and for taking corrective action and preventive action. The procedure(s) shall define requirements for

a) identifying and correcting nonconformity(ies) and taking action(s) to mitigate their environmental impacts,
b) investigating nonconformity(ies), determining their cause(s) and taking actions in order to avoid their recurrence,
c) evaluating the need for action(s) to prevent nonconformity(ies) and implementing appropriate actions designed to avoid their occurrence,
d) recording the results of corrective action(s) and preventive action(s) taken, and
e) reviewing the effectiveness of corrective action(s) and preventive action(s) taken.

Actions taken shall be appropriate to the magnitude of the problems and the environmental impacts encountered.

The organization shall ensure that any necessary changes are made to environmental management system documentation.

As a good business manager, you probably do these things already, even though you may not call them a "nonconformity assessment." The real question here is: Are you getting the environmental management job done? If not, why not?

Notice that "actions taken shall be appropriate to the magnitude of the problem and the environmental impacts encountered." No overkill is needed. If you have a little problem, fix it ("take corrective action") and move on. If you have big problem, get it resolved ("take corrective action"), devote the resources necessary to set things up so it never happens again ("take preventive action") and move on.

You may find problems either with the system (system performance) or with the results of the system's operation (environmental performance). The ISO 14004 guidance gives some examples:

---

a) system performance:
1) failure to establish environmental objectives and targets;
2) failure to define responsibilities required by an environmental management system, such as responsibilities for achieving objectives and targets or for emergency preparedness and response; and
3) failure to periodically evaluate compliance with legal requirements.

b) environmental performance:
1) energy reduction targets are not achieved;
2) maintenance requirements are not performed as scheduled; and
3) operating criteria (e.g. permitted limits) are not met.

In either case, take appropriate action, and move on.

Control of Records

"Records" and "documents" are not the same thing. Both must be controlled, but typically records relate to monitoring and audits, while documents relate to policies, procedures and operations. Why? Because, as you remember from the Control of Documents section, documents are often drafted, circulated for comment, revised, made available for use, revised as situations change, kept up to date, etc.

Records, on the other hand, are NOT revised. A *record* provides permanent evidence of ongoing operations; one "records" a particular state or result of the system, as it were. A record may contain measurements taken at a certain time or place; it may consist of photographs of a spill or leak or copies of notices published in newspapers or minutes of meetings. These kinds of documents don't get revised, they just get filed for future reference (such as during an audit).

The ISO 14001 requirement is short and sweet:

4.5.4 Control of records

The organization shall establish and maintain records as necessary to demonstrate conformity to the requirements of its environmental management system and of this International Standard, and the results achieved.

The organization shall establish, implement and maintain a procedure(s) for the identification, storage, protection, retrieval, retention and disposal of records.

Records shall be and remain legible, identifiable and traceable.

Because records have historical value – they record a specific event or time period – it is important to maintain them in such a way that they "remain legible, identifiable and traceable." **This means your computer records, too!**

I have a client with 25 years of computerized wildlife habitat monitoring records that are unusable because their format was never updated and they can't be read by today's computer software (does anyone even remember Data General, or that they made computers?). Luckily, they still have a warehouse full of boxes of the original field notes – on paper. Let this be a lesson!

Here's what kinds of records to keep control of (based on ISO 14004 guidance):

---

a) information on compliance with applicable legal requirements and other requirements to which the organization subscribes,
b) details of nonconformities and corrective and preventive actions,
c) results of environmental management system audits and management reviews,
d) information on environmental attributes of products (e.g. chemical composition and properties),
e) evidence of fulfillment of objectives/targets,
f) information on participation in training,
g) permits, licenses or other forms of legal authorization,
h) results of inspection and calibration activity, and
i) results of operational controls (maintenance, design, manufacture).

Internal Audit

Ah, the audit. What can I say about the audit, except that it is THE tool for ultimately figuring out whether what you are doing is working or not.

The ISO 14001 standard says:

4.5.5 Internal audit

The organization shall ensure that internal audits of the environmental management system are conducted at planned intervals to
a) determine whether the environmental management system
1) conforms to planned arrangements for environmental management including the requirements of this International Standard, and
2) has been properly implemented and is maintained, and
b) provide information on the results of audits to management.

Audit programme(s) shall be planned, established, implemented and maintained by the organization, taking into
consideration the environmental importance of the operation(s) concerned and the results of previous audits.

Audit procedure(s) shall be established, implemented and maintained that address
—the responsibilities and requirements for planning and conducting audits, reporting results and retaining associated records,
—the determination of audit criteria, scope, frequency and methods.

Selection of auditors and conduct of audits shall ensure objectivity and the impartiality of the audit process.

An auditor will collect "audit evidence" (records, statements of facts or other information) to compare against "audit criteria" (a set of policies, procedures or requirements), and prepare a list of "audit findings" (results of the evaluation of the collected evidence against the criteria).

What this means is that the auditor will plow around in your records and compare what s/he finds there against your policies and procedures, whatever industry or regulatory standards you have promised to abide by, and other aspects of your environmental policy. There is an entire ISO standard for auditing (ISO 14011), which you should acquire and study when you get this far along in your efforts; you will find it very useful if you decide to go ahead and get your enterprise certified to the ISO 14001 standard.

Question 5 – Did We Get There (and *now* where do we go)?

You are almost finished! In fact, you are finished with the design of the actual environmental management system; all that is left is to design a procedure for periodic (usually annual) review by *top management* (remember them? the ones whose fault it is if anything goes wrong?). On a day-to-day basis the worker bees usually keep things going just fine, but every once in a while it is important to get the big bosses involved in a formal way. In fact, ISO requires it.

The ISO 14001 standard puts it bluntly:

4.6 Management review

Top management shall review the organization's environmental management system, at planned intervals, to ensure its continuing suitability, adequacy and effectiveness. Reviews shall include assessing opportunities for improvement and the need for changes to the environmental management system, including the environmental policy and environmental objectives and targets. Records of the management reviews shall be retained.

Input to management reviews shall include
a) results of internal audits and evaluations of compliance with legal requirements and with other requirements to which the organization subscribes,
b) communication(s) from external interested parties, including complaints,
c) the environmental performance of the organization,
d) the extent to which objectives and targets have been met,
e) status of corrective and preventive actions,
f) follow-up actions from previous management reviews,
g) changing circumstances, including developments in legal and other requirements related to its environmental aspects, and
h) recommendations for improvement.

The outputs from management reviews shall include any decisions and actions related to possible changes to environmental policy, objectives, targets and other elements of the environmental management system, consistent with the commitment to continual improvement.

Notice that the criteria for the environmental management system are *suitability, adequacy, and effectiveness*. Is it suitable for the task (given the environmental aspects and impacts of your enterprise)? Is it adequate to do the job (does it have the resources, procedures and operational controls it needs)? Is it effective (are you actually reaching your objectives and meeting your targets?)

Here are the kinds of things top management should review (based on ISO 14004):

Inputs to the management review may include

a) results of internal audits and evaluations of compliance with applicable legal requirements and with other requirements to which the organization subscribes,
b) communication from external interested parties, including complaints,
c) the environmental performance of the organization,
d) the extent to which objectives and targets have been met,
e) status of corrective and preventive actions,
f) follow-up actions from previous management reviews,
g) changing circumstances, including
    1) changes in the organization's products, activities and services,
    2) results of the evaluation of environmental aspects from planned or new developments,
    3) changes in applicable legal requirements and other requirements to which the organization subscribes,
    4) the views of interested parties,
    5) advances in science and technology, and
    6) lessons learned from emergency situations and accidents,
h) recommendations for improvement.

Outputs from the review of the environmental management system may include decisions on

---

> —the system's suitability, adequacy and effectiveness,
> —changes to physical, human and financial resources, and
> —actions related to possible changes to environmental policy, objectives, targets and other elements of the environmental management system.

Of course, top management doesn't conduct this review alone, unless of course you are the entire management and staff of your enterprise. Even then, it would be nice to have some company. For larger enterprises, make sure to involve the environmental manager, department managers, key front-line staff (the groundskeeper, kitchen helper and janitor come to mind) and perhaps even representatives of the public, guests, regulators – whoever can help you determine whether the system got you where you wanted to be, and *where to go next.*

Because now you are at the most exciting point in your journey: the search for continual improvement.

What new objectives and targets can you set? Are there new topics about which you want to develop policies? Is there new technology to explore that will take you "beyond compliance" and perhaps keep you a step ahead of the competition? Can you create a partnership with environmental advocacy groups that will be mutually beneficial? Should you market your "green" accomplishments more, or differently than before?

Chapter 5 – Sustainability Principles

 We have installed our capable crew: our sustainability practices. We have built our sturdy ship: our sustainability processes, as documented in our environmental management system. Now it is time to discover our trusty compass, the tool that will guide us unerringly as we continue our ongoing sustainability journey. In the last chapter you learned how to answer the question, "Where do we want to go?" This chapter helps you answer the question, "Where is the *right place* to go?"

First, a little theory. It is important to understand the theory here; it will help everything else in this chapter make more sense. Because the term "sustainability" gets tossed around in a lot of different ways nowadays, it is valuable to know that there is a real-world, scientific basis for the sustainability principles I am about to discuss.

If you were going to create a "theoretical model of sustainability," where would you start? Karl-Henrik Robért, along with Herman Daly, Paul Hawken and John Holmberg (1997) began with what they called the "critical requirements," of which they identified eight:

1. The model must be based on a scientifically acceptable conception of the world.
2. The model must contain a scientifically supportable definition of sustainability.
3. The overall perspective must be applicable at different scales, and must see the economy as a subsystem of the ecosystem at each scale. Individuals must see how their actions aggregate from micro scales up to the macro scale, and thus understand their role in the overall move toward sustainability.
4. The micro-economical perspective should not require individuals to act against self interest. We may need some altruistic behaviour in the political task of setting up the rules of the game, but in the actual playing of the game we should not expect individuals to behave altruistically.
5. The model must be pedagogical and simple to disseminate so that it can support a public consensus necessary to be put into practice democratically.
6. The model must not engender unnecessary resistance or be adversarial.
7. The model must be able to get started without first requiring large scale societal changes. It should be implementable within today's economic reality. Business corporations, political parties and the public should be able to use the model directly.
8. It would be an advantage if the model also could be used as a starting point for developing "new economics" – as a way to recognize a new and larger pattern of scarcity to which old and basic economizing principles must be applied.

What's important for you to know here is that the set of principles that follows is based on those 8 criteria: the Natural Step principles are science-based, applicable at different scales, do not require altruism, are easy to teach, are simple to apply, and *you can start right now*.

They will serve as the compass for your journey.

The Four System Conditions

The Natural Step is based on 4 "non-negotiable" system conditions that describe how nature and society operate. They are non-negotiable in that we humans didn't create them and we cannot change them at our will. If we violate them through our actions (or inactions), they will continue to operate anyway, to our ultimate detriment. We – our societies, our businesses, our enterprises no matter how small or large – cannot hope to be sustainable without paying very close attention to them.

System Condition 1

Substances from the lithosphere must not systematically increase in the ecosphere.

This means that mineral matter (including both solid minerals such as iron, copper, gold, titanium and coal, and fluid minerals such as oil and gas) should not be extracted at a rate faster than they can be replenished in nature.

Clearly humans worldwide have already violated this condition; the practical question is, how can we slow the rate of extraction and dispersion in the future? Many of these materials, already extracted, processed and distributed, can be recycled almost infinitely (plastic, for example). Many manufactured items can be re-used or re-purposed in new uses so that virgin materials do not have to be extracted or processed to make new products.

Finally, you have a good scientific basis for adopting your recycling practices.

System Condition 2

Substances produced by society must not systematically increase in the ecosphere.

This means that natural materials that are processed such that nature cannot decompose them any longer (such as stainless steel as compared with iron), or artificial materials that cannot be broken down by nature at all (such as many persistent chemicals or byproducts of other processes, such as plutonium) should be managed so they do not increase beyond current levels. We have already seen the damage persistent materials such as mercury and lead can do to human health and communities.

So we need to find ways to re-use, re-purpose, or re-cycle manufactured items through rendering into their component parts, and phase out our use of persistent materials with no known method of ultimate decomposition.

System Condition 3

The physical basis for the productivity and diversity of nature must not be systematically deteriorated.

This means we must avoid over harvesting or manipulating aspects of our natural environment such that productivity and diversity deteriorate. As Karl-Henrik Robért points out, "Our health and prosperity depend on the capacity of nature to re-concentrate and restructure wastes into resources."

As I write this, the salmon fishery on the west coast of the US is closed for the season, due to a combination of over fishing, river modifications and climate change. The Three Gorges Dam in China has created a cesspool of toxic waters upstream, unusable for agriculture or drinking. More levees are breaking as rising waters of the Mississippi River seek their natural course through the river's floodplain, which just happens to be through cities and town and neighborhoods built in its path.

I think of this system condition as having an essential corollary: *Always remember, we do not control "nature," or natural processes.* For example, hotels built right on the beach in tsunami country are sitting ducks for disaster, however "sustainable" their kitchen practices or environmental management system might be, and this is as true in Oregon as it is in Sri Lanka.

System Condition 4

There must be fair and efficient use of resources with respect to meeting human needs.

All humans need shelter, food, water; most need clothing, transport, and productive work. How each of us uses resources, both as individuals and in our enterprises, affects every other human on the planet. Our task is to use them efficiently, so everyone can meet their basic human needs.

Remember the basic definition of sustainability is that which "meets the needs of the present without compromising the ability of future generations to meet their own needs." So System Condition 4 is the basic reason we seek sustainability at all, isn't it?

We have come full circle. As the poet T.S. Eliot said, "... the end of all our exploring will be to arrive where we started and know the place for the first time."

Applying the Conditions: Using the Compass

These four basic non-negotiable system conditions for organizations and for humans to survive – to be sustainable – translate into the following four decision-making principles:

1. The organization must systematically decrease its dependence on materials extracted from the lithosphere (for example, fossil fuels, metals, minerals and other non-renewable materials from the earth's crust)

2. The organization must systematically decrease its dependence on persistent unnatural substances (for example, man-made chemicals that do not biodegrade because they are exotic to nature and there are no natural mechanisms to degrade them)

3. The organization must systematically decrease its dependence on activities which encroach on productive parts of nature (for example, forests, rivers, wetlands, biodiversity – in other words, that harm the ecological systems that produce food, air, water necessary to human life)

4. The organization must systematically decrease its dependence on using large amounts of resources in relation to added human value (that is, that violate the basic principles of social equity).

An easy way to remember these four principles is what I call the "Four E's":

1. Extraction
2. Exotics
3. Ecology
4. Equity

Your enterprise should avoid activities that depend on the first two (extraction and exotics) and should undertake actions that protect and enhance the second two (ecology and equity).

How to Use the Compass

Like any shiny new tool, your new compass comes with an instruction manual. Unlike most instruction manuals, however, this one is really simple. It consists of only two steps:

1. Ask how your proposed decision (about adopting a practice, purchasing equipment or supplies, identifying environmental aspects or impacts, developing a policy, setting objectives and targets, creating a procedure, selecting new aspects to address as part of continual improvement – about anything you do) helps you meet each of the four system conditions, and take note of the answer.

2. Repeat.

Here's an example of how this works. In 1998 a colleague and I ran an exercise at a sustainability workshop where representatives of several major chemical and manufacturing corporations were in the same room as representatives from the state Department of Health, who enforced the statewide environmental and health regulations. All of them were asked to examine their day-to-day actions against these four sustainability principles, and discuss the results.

The Health Department representatives discovered to their horror that although they talked a good line, they actually had the worst performance of any group at the workshop. All they had done to try to be "sustainable" was to purchase recycled paper for the office copier! The others at least could describe the beginnings of their environmental management systems, and several manufacturers were already exploring closed-cycle and other cleaner production and lean manufacturing techniques to lessen their use of raw materials.

Here is the format for asking the questions in Step 1 (Step 2 you can figure out for yourself):

Will my proposed decision (practice, purchase, procedure, policy, etc.) help my enterprise:

1. **systematically decrease its dependence on materials extracted from the lithosphere?**

2. **systematically decrease its dependence on persistent unnatural substances?**

3. **systematically decrease its dependence on activities which encroach on productive parts of nature?**

> **4. systematically decrease its dependence on using large amounts of resources in relation to added human value?**

If the answers to any (or all four) of these questions is "no," you are automatically led to the fifth Big TNS Question:

Should I do this at all?

What else could you do instead, or how could you do this proposal differently, in order to get more (or all) "yes" answers?

So far I have talked about the finding the direction you do *not* want to go. A compass also is intended to help you find the places you *do* want to reach.

The same question with just two small word changes now serves as compass as well:

> *How could* **my proposed decision (practice, purchase, procedure, policy, etc.) help my enterprise:**
>
> 1. **systematically decrease its dependence on materials extracted from the lithosphere?**
>
> 2. **systematically decrease its dependence on persistent unnatural substances?**
>
> 3. **systematically decrease its dependence on activities which encroach on productive parts of nature?**
>
> 4. **systematically decrease its dependence on using large amounts of resources in relation to added human value?**

The classic published hospitality-related application of TNS, at the Skandic Hotel chain in Europe, is described in detail in Brian Natriss and Mary Altomare's book, *The Natural Step for Business*, revised and updated in 1999. Here is the short version.

In 1992, all 100 of the Skandic Hotels were in need of a makeover: the brand was tired, staff turnover was high, other chains had entered their market, and their facilities needed upgrading. A new CEO took the entire management team on a retreat, at which they adopted a new set of core values for the company focused on *omtanke*, a Swedish word meaning *profound caring*: for their customers, their co-workers, their shareholders, their communities, and their natural environment. The Natural Step provided the foundation for embodying this new approach.

Within 5 years, the chain was again profitable. Their newly-designed "eco-rooms" contained 97% recyclable furniture, floor coverings, guest linens, and guest amenities (soaps, shampoo). Their staff turnover dropped dramatically (most TNS companies report this). Both new and returning guests now went out of the way to stay at one of their hotels. The CEO told Natriss and Altomare that "TNS is the biggest team-building and customer loyalty program" they had ever had.

But this approach to sustainability can take place anywhere, in the developed or developing world, in enterprises large or small, regardless of the existence of recycling facilities, freeways, large quantities of investment capital, or a staff full of Ph.D.s.

All you need is a pencil and paper. Really.

Chapter 6 – Putting It All Together

You have the crew, the ship, and the compass. Now it's time to launch (or continue) your journey toward sustainability.

This chapter will give you three pencil-and-paper tools to help you do just that. They are called The Hospitality Forever™ Outcome Generator; The Backcasting Process Tool™; and the Kismet Process™.

All three tools are based on two ideas: (1) the idea that it is helpful to have an picture of the general contours of your destination before you start the journey, and (2) the idea that time is your friend. If you have completed some of the activities in earlier chapters (especially Practices and the first part of Processes), you will have much of the background information you'll need to complete these successfully.

Some of these tools may seem strange to you at first, but they all are tried-and-true, and have been applied in enterprises large and small over many years with powerful results. Here goes.

The Hospitality Forever™ Outcome Generator

Complete the form below, giving these 7 questions your most thoughtful responses. This activity can easily be done in a group, either with each person doing their own version then combining the results, or by simply eliciting responses from everyone at once. The sticky note method described in Chapter 3 also is a good tool to generate outcomes in a group.

Question 1 asks you to define your desired outcome. Notice that it doesn't ask for some vague "vision" statement ("We will be successful and sustainable and protect the environment"), but rather asks you to really describe specific characteristics of your enterprise when it is being as sustainable as you would like it to be. What will the buildings, the kitchen, the landscape, the guest rooms, the dining room look like? What will be happening there? How does your future differ from your present?

In other words, build an actual picture in your mind of what you will see; imagine what you will hear, and perhaps even taste and smell (fresh, local, organic vegetables, anyone?); and notice how it will feel to have accomplished your goals.

Sometimes I have groups develop an actual picture on flip chart or butcher paper posted on the wall. Even "non-artists" in the group usually can come up with a clear visual representation of what their sustainable future might look like.

Question 2 asks for evidence: how will you know you have accomplished your desired outcome? What will people say about your enterprise? How much money will it be making? Will you have a notebook containing your procedures? Will your emissions, or water usage, or use of persistent chemicals, or energy consumption, or use of raw materials be decreased? By how much? Will you have won some awards? Will you and your staff feel happier? Will you have less staff turnover?

Question 3 is about the context: under what circumstances will your enterprise be functioning sustainably? This is not an opening to give excuses ("after we have a 95% year-round occupancy rate and the physical plant is completely amortized") but rather an opportunity to notice the ongoing realities of your operations. And you need to be realistic because you need to achieve your outcome in the real world, not in some dreamland where everything is already perfect.

Question 4 asks you to reflect on the possible unintended consequences of your success. If you reduce staff turnover, how will that affect the number and quality of summer jobs you can offer local students? Many people believe that hang tag programs fail because the housekeeping staff are afraid that if there is less washing to do they will lose their jobs. Every thing we do has consequences; it's important to know both the good and the bad before choosing a specific course of action.

Question 5 asks you to look thoughtfully at the past, and notice any barriers that have gotten in the way of success in this endeavor. Often the biggest barrier from the past is "I never thought to do it before!" (and you've already broken that one). Most people find that lack of knowledge forms a bigger barrier than lack of money, time, or motivation. That's one reason staff training programs are so important: they can't do the work if they don't know *to* do it, or *how* to do it.

Question 6 asks you to notice resources you already have, that will be useful in obtaining your desired outcome. Sometimes people will overlook resources right under their noses (a dedicated staff, a solid budgeting system, a supporting clientele or community, a history of successful undertakings), believing wrongly that they can't even begin until they hire a consultant, or get a new computer system, or get full buy-in from corporate headquarters. (Yes, I know, Top Management buy-in is essential to ultimate success, but someone has to alert them to the possibility, right?) How much of what you need is right here, right now?

And **Question 7** asks about what *else* you will need on the journey: how much money, time, staff, organization, knowledge, buy-in do you need tomorrow to keep you going? Remember that part of putting together a *policy* includes designating enough resources to carry it out – here's an opportunity to begin to identify what you'll need for the rest of the journey.

The Hospitality Forever Outcome Generator™

Outcome Question	Answer
1. When your facility is functioning exactly as you want it to be, in a sustainable way for both the environment and your business, what will that be like?	
2. What *additional* kinds of evidence will you use to demonstrate that the facility is functioning sustainably? (For example, consider what kinds of actions you will be taking, how the facility will look, how people in your community will talk about it, what your profits will be like, how your staff will behave, what your customers will say)	
3. Under what specific circumstances, with what specific kinds of staff, investors, customers, regulations, etc. will your facility function sustainably?	
4. How will functioning sustainably affect other aspects of your business, your industry, your staff, other facilities in your company or organization, your relationships with suppliers, customers, regulators, permittors, general public, community and neighbors, media, etc.?	
5. What has stopped you from functioning as sustainably as you would like to, in the past?	
6. What resources do you already have that will help you to function as sustainably as you would like to in the future?	
7. What other resources do you need in order to function as sustainably as you would like to in the future?	

The Backcasting Process Tool

Yes, you read it right: backcasting. It's simply the opposite of forecasting, a task we all engage in all the time. You forecast budgets, customer numbers and satisfaction levels, staffing needs, energy costs, high tides, fishing success, numbers of bottles of single-malt scotch to buy, all based on assumptions about what the future holds.

Why not simply go to that future and find out? Lots of people from IKEA and Skandic Hotels and Collins Pine and Interface have already done this, and reaped its benefits. Here's how to visit the future without a technological time machine.

The process itself is deceptively simple; once you try it, you'll know for yourself how powerful it can be. This process usually is done one person at a time (with a helper reading the steps aloud), but it would be interesting to try it with a group.

First, lay out a "timeline" on the floor with masking tape or string; it should be at least 10 meters long, in a straight line. This represents the period of time from "now" to the future, when you have accomplished your goal. Say the goal is to have developed a complete environmental management system, and you expect to have accomplished that in 24 months. So one end of the timeline represents today, and the other end represents that time 2 years from now when you have reached your goal.

Second, stand at the "now" end of the line, and look ahead at that future goal. Notice what you see, hear, and feel about that future (the results of the Outcome Generator can be very helpful here). Don't rush this step, make sure you take the time to get a full-body representation of that future. You may want to write some notes, if you haven't already.

Third, walk slowly toward the "future" end of the timeline, being very aware of ideas or insights that may arise while you walk. Write them down, if there are any.

Fourth, when you have reached the "future" turn around and look back along the timeline. This is the opportunity to notice all those little actions along the way that culminated in achieving your goal. What exactly happened? Who participated? Can you identify resources from this perspective that you didn't notice before? Does the path go in a straight line, or does it zig and zag in some way? Are their branches that enter or leave the path? How are events distributed through time: are there more at the beginning or at the end, or are they evenly spaced? Write down your observations.

Fifth, walk slowly back to "now" noticing as you do how the journey seems different from this direction. Write down any new insights, ideas, or observations.

Sixth, turn and look at the future, and notice how that is for you now: what do you see, hear, feel? What do you notice about the journey from "here" to "there" now? Write down your observations.

The Kismet Process™

The Kismet Process™ is a tool for identifying specific action steps and powerful organizational resources to achieve your desired future sustainable business reality. Based on a process developed by Leslie Cameron-Bandler, David Gordon and Michael Lebeau in the 1980s, it uses your knowledge of your own past business history to create a compelling future for your business as a leader in your industry.

Some of the specific exercises called for in this activity may seem unfamiliar at first, but as you learn and practice them you will acquire the ability to generate compelling futures that will serve you well in many areas of your business life.

It is best if you do this activity as a team, writing down the answers in the space provided. When your desired future has happened, it will be interesting to look back at your notes here and notice which parts of the activity were most helpful in creating it.

Step One: Developing an Image of the Future Business

The first step is to create a visual representation of your future sustainable business, 5 years from now. You know it will be older, and you expect it will be successful.

What will the physical facilities look like? You might want to begin by imagining the facilities aging as if you were in one of those motion pictures where the star grows older during the story. How would they look? Notice the landscape changing, perhaps the vegetation or plantings will change, perhaps other changes will occur. Will you have added anything? Taken anything away? If you have done the previous activities, you'll have some good material to start this one.

Now imagine other parts of your business: the staff, your vendors and suppliers, your customers and clients. How have they changed?

What about your balance sheet? Look at it now, the numbers at the bottom, how they have changed over the years.

See yourself in the picture: notice your clothes, how you sit or stand or move around, any associated artifacts (such as your desk, a briefcase, computer or phone, tools, etc.), and anything else you need to make a full and rich picture of you in your business as it will be in the future.

Remember to ask yourself how much profit is desirable? What will your customers and clients say about you? Will you be an industry leader? How will it feel to come to work each day?

Step Two: What Does the Future Business Want from You?

Now imagine it is 5 years into the future and imagine the business from that time right in front of you now. See it clearly, the facilities, the income stream, the publicity and customer comments, your landscape or offices, your energy bill, your staff and their actions -- make it all as vivid as you can.

Imagine actually moving into that future business, actually *being* the business, feeling what it feels, seeing what it sees, hearing what it hears. Notice what it's like to be that much older, that successful, hearing people say what they say about you. Your experience during the Backcasting activity will be helpful here.

Move back out of the future, and ask your future business: "What do you want from me now?" You will get a sense of an answer, perhaps in words, perhaps in images or sounds or feelings. Sometimes you get a picture of what the future looks like. Sometimes it is a feeling of pride, success, happiness. You may hear stirring music, or a soft romantic ballad. You may even see a list, as one client did!

Whatever it is, write (or sketch) the answer below.

What Does Your Future Business Want from You?

Step Three: Conduct a Present Assessment

Conduct an assessment of your business today, in the present. Include both positive and negative items, and be sure to look at all the characteristics of successful businesses: profit, management, facilities, staff, relationships with vendors and customers, community participation, etc. Remember aspects and impacts? Some of that information will be helpful here.

Present Assessment	
• Profit	
• Management	
• Facilities	
• Staff	
• Vendor relationships	
• Client relationships	
• Community	
• Environment	

Step Four: Noticing How Far You've Come

Now conduct the same assessment for your business as it was <u>five years ago</u>. You may notice that some parts of your business have not changed very much, and some parts have changed dramatically (some for the better, some for the worse).

Past Assessment	
• Profit	
• Management	
• Facilities	
• Staff	
• Vendor relationships	
• Client relationships	
• Community	
• Environment	

Step Five: How Did You Get Here from There?

In this step you determine *how the specific actions you have taken (or not taken) in your business over the past 5 years* have contributed to creating your present situation. You may notice things you have done, or not done, ideas you have used, or not used, investments you have made, or not made. Whether you interpret them as positive or negative, make a list of what you did to create "now":

_____

_____

_____

_____

_____

_____

_____

_____

_____

_____

_____

_____

_____

_____

_____

_____

Step Six: How Could The Present Situation Have Been Worse?

Imagine how your business could have been in a much *worse* situation today if these actions had been different in the past 5 years. You may think of some actions that were merely inappropriate, or of decisions that were impulsive, irresponsible, etc. Perhaps there was no systematic plan, or no analysis of potential unintended consequences. The point here is not to judge, but simply to notice in a different way how these past actions have affected your current situation.

_____

_____

_____

_____

_____

_____

_____

_____

_____

_____

_____

_____

_____

_____

_____

_____

_____

Step Seven: How Could The Present Situation Have Been Better?

Imagine what could have been done differently during the past 5 years to make the present situation even better than it is now. For example, if the business had invested in new or upgraded facilities, or energy-saving equipment; or if you had included your suppliers in your planning so you never needed to worry about running low on materials; or if relationships with your customers were improved so that you had so many referrals you could save considerably on your advertising budget. You know what evidence is important, that would demonstrate how the present situation could be even better than it is.

_____

_____

_____

_____

_____

_____

_____

_____

_____

_____

_____

_____

_____

_____

_____

Step Eight: Two Pictures of the Future

Now develop a visual representation of two possible futures 5 years from now:

1. one that you definitely *do* want, where your business is as successful and profitable and sustainable as you want it to be

2. one that you definitely do *not* want, where your business is losing money and customers and your facilities and environment have deteriorated beyond repair

Imagine in your mind how it would be to be in either of these futures, first the one you want, then the one you do not want. Be sure to make these representations as complete as possible: what will you see, hear, feel? who is with you? what are the surroundings like? what are you doing? This is a very important step, so take the time to do it completely.

You might want to imagine some "special effects" like in the movies: certain colors or sounds or smells that are particularly attractive to you (for the desired future) or repulsive to you (for the undesirable future). Make the images in 3-D, big and bright and up close, perhaps using special movements or multiple screens. The purpose is to make each of these potential futures as real to you as possible.

You can make some notes here about these images, if you want:

1. Desired Future

_____

_____

_____

_____

_____

2. Undesired Future

_____

_____

_____

_____

Step Nine: Behaviors That Lead to Your Desired Future

Now ask, "How can we get the future business we want?" Make sure that any actions you think of are under your direct control, not subject to the control (or whim) of others. For example, "having the bank give me lots of money for my program" or "having my staff like me" may be helpful, but focus on what actions you and the business itself can take to help these things come to pass. If you don't have enough information to know right now, ask "How can I learn what I need to make it happen?" These actions are *actions worth doing* and you need to list them here for reference:

_____

_____

_____

_____

_____

_____

_____

_____

_____

_____

_____

_____

_____

_____

_____

_____

Step Ten: Behaviors That Lead to Your Undesirable Future

Identify behaviors that will lead to your undesirable future. These will be *actions to avoid*. List them below:

_____

_____

_____

_____

_____

_____

_____

_____

_____

_____

_____

_____

_____

_____

_____

_____

_____

_____

Final Step: Understanding Your Resources

Now you have vivid representations of desirable and undesirable futures, and you know which actions will lead to which one. These representations, and your lists of actions, are powerful resources for you, for your present and future business, and for your whole team. Review these lists of *actions worth doing* and *actions to avoid* at least during your annual management review, as a reality check during the future development. You will immediately notice which future you are heading toward, and can take any necessary steps to reorient your planning. Each time you take an *action worth doing* make sure you appreciate your activity: congratulate the whole team because you can feel and see your business approaching your desired future. Of course, if you were to engage in an *action to avoid* you would feel and see yourself approaching your undesirable future, and can change your behavior accordingly.

Note here any additional resources, ideas and actions you need to ensure your desired future:

Some Notes on the Real World

How real is all this? What are the pitfalls and warnings everyone should know before they begin this journey to sustainability?

It is possible to go from ground zero to ISO 14001 certification in about 12 months for a resort of about 100 rooms. "Sustainability," of course, is a concept that requires ongoing effort, commitment, and involvement from top management, all the staff, and those with whom the enterprise interacts (customers, public, regulators, industry associations). Enterprises that have adopted The Natural Step principles as their compass typically report continued enthusiasm from staff, customers and investors after decades of being underway.

Smaller or larger facilities do not necessarily require much less, or much more, time, as most of the same departments and functions must be handled. The staff training program for a larger facility will take longer to complete than for a smaller one, and some of the actual environmental actions on the action program will be proportionately more time consuming and costly (installing electricity meters for each guest room, for example). But there are often economies of scale, also, in larger facilities or for enterprises with many facilities (chains or franchises).

Most resorts in both the developed and the developing world have very hard-working and diligent staffs, who are fully employed in doing their current jobs. Therefore, adding some new tasks related to developing environmental objectives and targets, writing down procedures, measuring results, and reviewing programs may seem overwhelming at first. This is especially likely to be true if principal staff are not fully aware at the outset of the implementation effort of all that will be expected of them in the coming months.

Therefore, I strongly recommend that top management and all principal staff participate in an active introductory training, along the lines of our *Sustainability for the Hospitality Industry* workshop. This two-day overview workshop is conducted on site and includes hands-on exercises that accomplish the following results:

- it acquaints everyone with the basic concepts of sustainability, including the contents of the ISO 14001 environmental management system standard
- it helps everyone understand how the three parts to sustainability, (Practices, Processes and Principles) will affect their job and their department
- it allows participants to determine for themselves their needs for time, money, and data during implementation
- it ensures top management supports and participates in the program

At this time everyone's initial questions can be answered, and the management and staff will have a more realistic idea of what specific actions and time frames will be needed to achieve certification.

Issues that may arise during implementation of a sustainability program may include many management issues related to collaborative decision-making and to record keeping, especially in the developing world. Many hotels and resorts in general are more familiar with top-down systems of management, and many keep written records of their day-to-day operations only informally, if they keep them at all. This is especially true of the smaller, one-owner or family-owned establishments, but some units of quite large chains also operate this way, either overall or in certain departments. This is just as true of a chain unit in St. Louis as it is of a guest house in Phuket.

While any facility can choose to adopt a few sustainable practices without much inter-departmental collaboration or formal documentation, developing an environmental management system that conforms to the ISO 14001 standard will highlight these management issues, and will provide a wonderful opportunity to clarify and systematize the entire operation, from the front office to the garden.

Frequently Asked Questions

Doesn't it take a lot of time and effort to do this, in addition to our regular job?

Yes, of course it does. But remember, these early activities (developing a policy, identifying aspects and impacts, developing objectives and targets, writing procedures, etc.) need only to be done once for the entire operation. Periodic reviews will result in small changes to those parts of the system that require fine-tuning; the initial comprehensive study and analysis will not have to be repeated.

We are not professional trainers; how can we train our employees?

Facility staff are often the best trainers, because they know the specific issues and personalities and barriers far better than anyone from outside. By conducting in-house Train-the-Trainer sessions, you can teach your own staff to provide peer-to-peer training on every facet of your sustainability program. IKEA, for example, trained 600 of its own employees worldwide to do its own sustainability training.

Our departments are not familiar with talking to each other this much.

Get used to it! You should make sure there is a way for everyone to have input when needed. And be respectful of people's time: not everyone has to meet with everyone else all the time. If Purchasing and Housekeeping need to talk, they should meet together and talk.

Whose responsibility is it to accomplish this certification, if we decide to go for it?

Everyone can (and should) help, but Top Management is ultimately responsible.

Whose job is it to manage the environmental management system?

Someone should be assigned this task, usually in a position called "Environmental Manager." But everyone can (and should) participate, including Top Management.

We need formats, templates, models to follow; this will make our lives easier!

Yes, I agree. You can download printable copies of all the formats, templates and models in this book from our web site at http://www.hospitalityforever.com

Some of our employees are not fluent in written or spoken English (or French, or Spanish, or Bahasa, or Persian, or Afrikaans)

No problem. Just make sure their training, and your policies, procedures, and other written documents are provided in the language(s) they *are* fluent in. People cannot do what they do not understand. The Competence, Training and Awareness part of your system should be designed to take care of this problem.

We are confused about what is environmental *performance* and what is an environmental management *system*

An *environmental management system* means the part of the overall management system for the enterprise that includes organizational structure, planning activities, responsibilities, practices, procedures, processes and resources for developing, implementing, achieving, reviewing and maintaining the organization's environmental policy.

Environmental performance means the results of an organization's management of its environmental aspects, as measured against its environmental policy, objectives and targets.

So the system is how you get the performance; the performance is the result of the system.

We can't possibly be ready for a certification audit within 12 months!

Sure you can. Others have done it, and so can you. And remember, you can choose whether or not to go for certification. Many organizations develop wonderful environmental management systems and never choose to get certified. The criterion is what works best for *you*.

We have no national environmental regulatory framework within which to evaluate "significance" of our aspects and impacts

Then you get to determine significance for yourselves. While you may not need to (or be able to) measure parts per million of some hazardous contaminant in your groundwater, you can measure basic qualities and compare them against World Health Organization standards, for example. Or you can determine for yourself that a certain number of acres removed from production in the nearby forest each year is too many, and take steps through your sustainability program to decrease your contribution to that. The advantage of the tools outlined in this book is that they are voluntary, private sector tools that give you a lot of control over your own destiny and that of your business and your community.

Writing things down this way is unfamiliar to us and to our employees

I know. Remember that even under the ISO 14001 standard, you get to determine what parts of you system need to be documented, and how to control those documents. Start small, and grow only as you need to. Sustainability isn't a paperwork exercise – in fact, you may set a target to reduce your use of paper, yes?

I want to do my part but my department doesn't have a significant impact

Then cheer on the rest of the team! Your ideas are still welcome; maybe your department can take up some of the slack, or because of your unique perspective you can notice impacts others have been blind to.

Our water treatment plant is not yet on line; can we still get certified?

Yes, if you want to. Remember that under the ISO 14001 standard, you get to choose the "scope" of your environmental management system. You can begin your process without your water treatment plant (as long as you are in compliance with all applicable water quality requirements), then add that function to your system as it comes on line.

My facility is just one unit in a large chain; how do I get started without top management support or approval?

You can simply begin. Start with those activities that do not need approval, and document your results from Day One (cost savings, resource savings, employee morale, customer comments, etc.). Gradually your example can help convince corporate executives to take notice, and find a way to install these practices, processes and principles throughout the organization.

Do we have to do everything all at once, or can we save some actions for continuous improvement?

You know the answer to that one, now, don't you?

References and Resources

Books and Other Print Resources

American Hotel and Motel Association, *Environmental Action Pack for Hotels,* 1996

Anderson, Ray, *Midcourse Correction,* Peregrinzilla Press, 1999

Blackburn, William R., *The Sustainability Handbook,* Environmental Law Institute, 2008

Block, Marilyn R., *Identifying Environmental Aspects and Impacts,* ASQ Quality Press, 1999

Cameron-Bandler, Leslie, David Gordon and Michael Lebeau, *Know How,* Futurepeace, 1986

Cascio, Joseph, *ISO 14000 Handbook,* ASQ Quality Press, 1999

Elkington, John, *Cannibals with Forks,* Capstone Publishing Ltd., 1999

Hawken, Paul, *The Ecology of Commerce,* Harper Business, 1994

Kuhre, W. Lee, *ISI 14001 Certification,* Prentice Hall ,1995

Natriss, Brian and Mary Altomare, *The Natural Step for Business,* New Society Publishers, 1999

Robért, Karl-Henrik, *The Natural Step Story,* New Society Publishers, 2002

Robért, Karl-Henrik, Herman Daly, Paul Hawken, and John Holmberg, *A Compass for Sustainable Development,* The Natural Step, 1997

Stipanuk, David, and Harold Roffman, *Hospitality Facilities Management and Design,* Education Institute, American Hotel and Motel Association, 1996

Tibor, Tom, *Implementing ISO 14000,* McGraw Hill, 1996

UN World Commission on Environment and Development, *Our Common Future,* 1987

Internet Resources

American Hotel and Lodging Association (formerly American Hotel & Motel Association)	www.ahla.com
Conservation International	www.conservation.org
Environmental Training & Consulting International, Inc.	www.envirotrain.com
Green Globe	www.greenglobe.org
Green Hotels Association	www.greenhotels.com
Green Meetings Industry Council	www.greenmeetings.info
Green Restaurant Association	www.dinegreen.com
Green Seal	www.greenseal.org
Hospitality Forever program of ETCI	www.hospitalityforever.com
International Ecotourism Society	www.ecotourism.org
International Hotel and Restaurant Association	www.ih-ra.com
International Hotels Environment Initiative	www.ihei.org
International Organization for Standardization (ISO)	www.iso.org.ch
National Ski Areas Association	www.nsaa.org
Oceans Blue Foundation	www.oceansblue.org
The Natural Step	www.naturalstep.org
United Nations Environment Programme	www.unep.org
World Health Organization	www.who.int
World Tourism Organization	www.world-tourism.org
World Travel and Tourism Council	www.wttc.org
Worldwide Fund for Animals	www.worldwildlife.org

This book is one of an ongoing series of environmental "how to" handbooks, white papers, and
checklist collections published for

Environmental Training & Consulting International, Inc.
1970 NW Overton, Suite 100
Portland, OR 97209 USA
Voice 503-274-1790
Fax 503-274-1791
http://www.envirotrain.com
info@envirotrain.com

ETCI is the USA's premier provider of custom-designed, in-house environmental training on environmental impact assessment, environmental management systems, and sustainability.

Contact us to discuss scheduling a live on-site workshop for your organization.

For downloadable copies of all worksheets, templates, and forms in this book, visit

http://www.hospitalityforever.com

About the Author

Leslie E. Wildesen, Ph.D., is an environmental scientist with over 40 years' experience as a researcher, project planner, program manager, consultant and trainer. She has conducted environmental and business sustainability projects throughout the US, as well as in Asia, Latin America, and Africa. She lives in Portland, Oregon, USA.